THE
ASCENT
OF THE
MOUNTAIN OF GOD

THE ASCENT

OF THE

MOUNTAIN OF GOD

Daily Reflections
for the Journey of Lent

EDWARD HAYS

FOREST OF PEACE Notre Dame, Indiana

Other Books by the Author:
(available from Forest of Peace)

Prayers and Rituals
Prayers for a Planetary Pilgrim
Prayers for the Domestic Church
Prayers for the Servants of God

Contemporary Spirituality
The Lenten Labyrinth
Holy Fools & Mad Hatters
A Pilgrim's Almanac
Pray All Ways
Secular Sanctity
In Pursuit of the Great White Rabbit

Parables and Stories
The Quest for the Flaming Pearl
St. George and the Dragon
The Magic Lantern
The Ethiopian Tattoo Shop
Twelve and One-Half Keys
Sundancer
The Christmas Eve Storyteller

The Ascent of the Mountain of God

copyright ©1994, by Edward M. Hays

ISBN: 0-939516-26-8

Dedicated to

Archbishop James Patrick Keleher

for his support and affirmation
of the Ministry of Contemplative Prayer

Contents

Come, let us climb God's Mountain

– Isaiah 2: 3

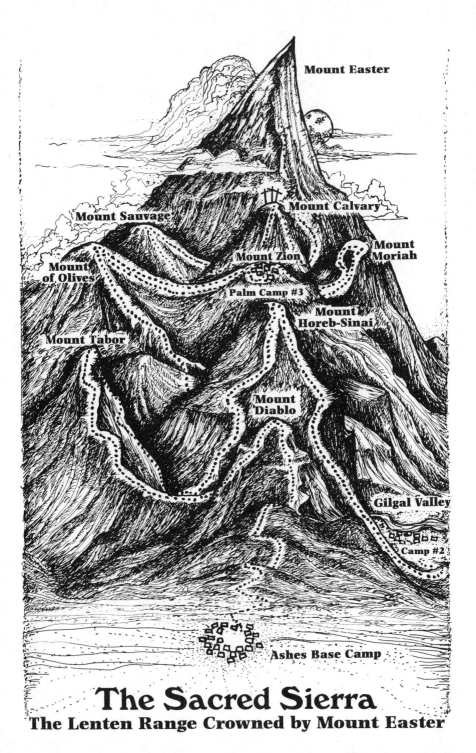

The Sacred Sierra
The Lenten Range Crowned by Mount Easter

Preface
The Mountain of God

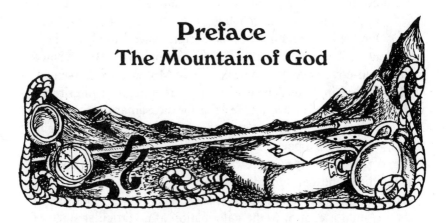

Global, truly catholic, is the image of the mountain in conveying the presence of God. A tall mountain, rising out of the flat plains—out of the ordinary level of human affairs—and seemingly touching the heavens, has been a universal religious symbol. In all cultures, it has been the home or meeting place for the gods or God. Among the sacred mountains of the world are Mounts Fuji, Elbrus, Sinai, Sauvage, Horeb, Tabor, Tlaloc, Carmel, Gerizim, Kailas and Olympus.

Most of these holy peaks have had a particular aura about them that has heightened their sense of sacredness. The clouds that surround these mountaintops have inspired many an imagination. When a particular sacred mountain is also a volcano, there is an even greater sense of awe.

The cosmos itself was seen by the ancients as a terraced mountain. That vision provided the blueprint for pyramids in Mesopotamia, Egypt, Mexico, China, India and elsewhere. Scholars believe that around such artificially constructed holy mountains sprang up the first cities and the roots of civilization. Over the ages these architectural holy mountains as well as their natural counterparts have become the destination of countless religious pilgrimages. In Japan, for example, every year 200,000 pilgrims climb to the top of Mount Fuji.

Poets like Dante and mystics like St. John of the Cross have seen mountains as images of the spiritual journey to God. St. John called his path to God *The Ascent of Mount Carmel*. Artists have pictured the Last Judgment as Christ seated on a high mountain with all the other mountains having been symbolically leveled.

Our Jewish-Christian-Islamic Scriptures are filled with holy mountains. The great archetype is Mount Sinai, where God visited the cloud-covered volcanic peak to give Moses a new covenant. Mount Zion in Jerusalem was the holy mountain of pilgrimage for the Jews, as was Mount Gerizim for the Samaritans.

While the name *mount* can at times imply a small mountain, it is in fact more a poetic title than an indication of size. Some of the world's tallest peaks are called mounts, with Mount Everest being the highest among the towering peaks of the Himalayas. In religious literature a *mount* usually refers to the very pinnacle of the spiritual ascent or to the culmination of a particular stage of the journey. In Scripture, Mounts Sinai, Gilead, Ebal, Hermon and Carmel, the Mount of Olives and Mount Calvary provide us with vivid images of significant steps along the ascent of holy individuals and the whole people of God.

Likewise, the Lenten pilgrimage has several mounts that need to be scaled along the way of the sacred sierra. Beginning on Ash Wednesday and with each week of Lent, *The Mountain of God* will lead you to another height on the range crowned by Mount Easter. This manual for holy mountain climbing provides tools, allies and insights that will turn the challenge into an adventure and enhance the joy of the journey.

Monday Before Ash Wednesday
Preparation for the Ascent

Lent is a pilgrimage to a mystic holy mountain. As with Moses, it is an ascent to a mountaintop meeting with the Divine Mystery. Isaiah addressed this invitation to everyone willing to embrace the adventure of the ascent of God's mountain: "Come, let us climb God's mountain" (Is. 2: 3).

For mystics, the path to God has always been like climbing a mountain. It is an ascent, a rising up to a higher and holier life. This quest to the summit of all we can be, and all we truly are, is a step-by-step ascent. As such, it requires reflection and preparation.

While deeply personal, it is also communal. Like mountain climbing, no mountain pilgrimages can be private or solitary exercises. Only a fool climbs a mountain alone. The scalings of great heights like Mount Everest are all done as expeditions—so should your Lenten ascent.

This pre-Lenten section of your handbook for holy mountain climbing deals with the preparation for your ascent. As you climb, it will guide you step-by-step, day-by-day, along the path of the sacred Lenten mountain range. While the destination is Mount Easter, to reach the pinnacle will require climbing other mountains that form the sacred sierra. Among these are Mount Tabor, Mount Hermon, Mount Diablo and Mount Calvary.

Mountain climbing is a great adventure, yet it is no picnic. On this Monday before Ash Wednesday, reflect on whether you are prepared for such an expedition. Neither your age nor your state of health is an issue—neither can be an excuse to stay home. The most critical issue lies within your heart. Are you willing to invest it fully in this great adventure?

You can choose your Lenten works, your allies for the ascent now, before Ash Wednesday. Or perhaps you could begin this task now and complete it by Ash Saturday, the eve of the first Sunday in this season of reform and renewal. The next page of this mountaineer manual allows space for you to list your allies or spiritual works.

Allies for the Ascent
Lenten Works and Practices

The classic works of this season are acts of self-denial, fasting and abstinence, spiritual reading, acts of charity and daily attendance at the Eucharist or Lenten devotions.

The purpose of any Lenten work is to assist your ascent toward Mount Easter, the first step of which requires a change of heart. You may wish to pencil in your choices of Lenten practices that you hope will aid that inner transformation. As you read the coming pages of this mountain-climbing manual, your allies may change.

1.

2.

3.

4.

5.

O God, come to my assistance. O Lord, make haste to help me as I take up my Lenten allies, and my cross, to climb your holy mountain.

Tuesday Before Ash Wednesday
Preparation for the Expedition

Typical of the ascents of great mountains, this mountain-climbing expedition begins at a base camp. This is a place to be outfitted with the necessary provisions for the long climb up the mountain. It will actually take you forty-six days to reach the top of Mount Easter, if you count Sundays. While they are not usually included among the days of Lent (forty being a symbolic Scriptural number), for the majority of those journeying to Easter, Sundays are the only days of communal worship. Lenten Sundays are the "camps" where we come together with other climbers to chart our course and to find the mutual encouragement we need to continue. They are occasions to be aware that our ascent is no private exercise.

Today, on the Tuesday before Ash Wednesday, as you pack your gear for the ascent, be sure to include your Bible along with this mountain manual. Since the Mountain of God is approached from all sides by a global pilgrimage-expedition, each day's reflection in this book will refer to the Scripture readings used by various Christian denominations in their daily Lenten Liturgies.

If you are able to attend daily Eucharist, this book can become part of your preparation for the liturgical experience or an echo-recollection at day's end. If, like most of us, your work and family responsibilities do not permit such participation, your reading of the Scripture texts and your reflection on them will allow you to be in solidarity with the global expedition.

Yet even without the daily Scripture readings at hand, this manual will guide you along the mountain path. Each day's reflection begins with a capsule comment on the readings of the day, usually containing some advice for the ascent from one of the prophets or from the Gospel's Master Climber himself.

Today's Scripture text from Psalm 24, verses 3-4, provides a critical reflection as you prepare for the expedition. It asks who can ascend the Mountain of God and then answers: those with *sinless hands* and *clean hearts*, those *who don't desire what is vain* and *haven't sworn so as to deceive their neighbors.*

Like anyone who packs for a long journey, remind yourself of the cardinal rule of major expeditions: Travel as lightly as possible. Excessive baggage on an expedition such as this—baggage that you and you alone must carry—is indeed a drawback that will make the ascent difficult, if not impossible!

These days before Ash Wednesday are reconciliation days that call you to lighten the load. Examine your heart and unpack. Cleanse it of resentments and grudges, shame, guilt, fear, dead-end desires and heavy-handed ways of dealing with others. Jettison any excess emotional baggage. The preface of Lent, these holy days before Ash Wednesday, is the time to be cleansed of sins—and not during Holy Week, when most of the ascent will have taken place without you.

A New Mardi Gras Exercise

Today is *Mardi Gras*, French for "Fat Tuesday." Traditionally it's a day of carnival festivals and parties. Instead of weighing yourself down this year with a wild spree of eating, drinking and entertainment, a kind of last-night party, spend it in a serious journey into your heart. Are you too "fat"? Unload your heart of all that might cause you to collapse before you reach the glorious peak of Mount Easter.

Today, either by sacred ritual or in private prayer, ask to be forgiven of all that might hold you back in being reconciled to others and to God. Be prepared to administer the most difficult of all pardons, the forgiveness of yourself. This absolution is essential in being able to forgive those who have offended you or even to receive God's ever-present and unconditional pardon.

With reverence, remove all that's dark and heavy in your heart and soul as you cleanse yourself on the eve of the expedition.

Ritual-Prayer of Pardon

After careful and prayerful reflection, seek reconciliation in a ritualized way or perform a private prayer-ritual. If this is a communal-household prayer, each person is encouraged to spend time in silent examination. Place a bowl of water at the family table or in your prayer corner.

Prayer Before the Water Ritual

O God, you who are an endless ocean of mercy,
  whose compassion and never-failing love
  reaches higher than the heavens,
  cleanse me of all my failings to love.
Cleanse me of all shame for past mistakes
  as you rinse away all my dead-end desires,
  my heavy-handedness with others
  and the grime of my grudges.
Cleanse my heart with the blood of the Lamb,
  risen and glorious,
  so that with clean hands I may pick up my cross
  and with a light heart
  I may begin the ascent of your holy mountain.

Sacred Gesture: Dipping your fingers in the bowl of water, symbolically wash your face and your heart, or make the sign of the cross as you pray: *May the peace of Christ which flows from the cross be in my heart and soul. Amen.*

Ash Wednesday
Base Camp

The Prophet Joel tells us that God desires us to return with our whole hearts, that we are to rend our hearts, not our garments, and return to God (see Jl. 2: 12-18).

Jesus advises that whenever we pray, we are to go to our rooms, close our doors and pray to God in private (see Mt. 6: 1-6, 16-18).

Today we gather in the base camp to begin Lent. At the same time, Jesus calls you into your private tent to pray to God. That private prayer chamber you are invited to enter is your heart. Because of the call of Jesus and that of the prophet Joel, today might better be named Heart Wednesday than Ash Wednesday.

As a disciple, you are commissioned in the secret service of others—in acts of charity. You are also called to secret penance and to secret prayer. In the secrecy of your heart, explore your Lenten Luggage again and be sure that you're free of excess baggage. How easily we can leave on this journey with a heavy heart. Insofar as it is possible on this Ash Wednesday, jettison all that would prevent you from being clean of heart.

To signify that you are a member of the Lenten expedition of mountaineers on the ascent of the Mountain of God, you are given two signs: the mark of holy ashes and the bookmark of a blue ribbon that came with this book. The sign of the ashes, of course, is the traditional symbol for those embracing penance. The significance of your blue bookmark ribbon will be explained shortly.

Reflection

On this Ash Wednesday, reflect on an experience from the life of former President Jimmy Carter. He had applied to enter a nuclear submarine program under Admiral Hyman Rickover, who then interviewed him for the position. At the end of the interview Admiral Rickover asked, "How did you stand in your class at the Naval Academy?"

Carter answered, "Sir, I stood 59 in a class of 820," waiting to be congratulated.

Instead he was asked, "Did you do your best?"

Carter began to reply, "Yes, sir," but recalled that he could have learned more and so answered, "No, sir, I didn't always do my best."

Rickover looked at Carter for a long time in silence and then asked one final question, which Carter said he never forgot—nor was he able to answer—"Why not?"

Ask yourself if it is your intention today to enter into this Lenten season with a desire to do your best to make this truly an ascent to greatness and holiness. Ask yourself if you seek to be engaged during these forty holy days with such a passionate commitment that it will become the best Lent of your entire life. If that is not your intention, then ask yourself, "Why not?"

Ash Thursday

Today, one of history's most famous mountain climbers, Moses, sets before the Israelite community—and each of us—a clear choice: life or death (see Dt. 30: 15-20).

Jesus tells us that all who wish to be his followers must deny their very selves, take up their crosses each day, and follow in his footsteps (see Lk. 9: 22-25).

Moses the mountaineer scaled Mount Sinai to encounter God.

We, along with that original Exodus expedition, are challenged to "choose between life and death." His chilling choice reminds us of yesterday's ashes of death and their warning not to waste time. Death is a close companion to you and to everyone else on this expedition.

Because of that fearful specter, we would be well advised to take along more than the usual mountain-climbing equipment. It would be wise to take up the usual brightly colored avalanche cord (in case we are buried beneath ice or rock), brake bars, ice hammers, crampons (toothed metal boot attachments to increase traction), ropes and harnesses. And, paradoxically, to ensure our survival, we need to take up our crosses!

Jesus says, "Follow me"—to which might be added, "rope yourself to me, and to one another, as we prepare for the ascent." Previously the season of Lent has been viewed as a time for personal spiritual exercises and private devotions. The new Lent calls for a constant awareness that this is a communal ascent, a journey with those with whom we live and worship and with the global Christian community.

These days after Ash Wednesday and prior to the First Sunday of Lent are important for those who are truly serious about this journey. They provide an opportunity to ponder our destination and how we can achieve the summit of Easter. These are days to dedicate and rededicate yourself to do your best with the various exercises, allies and equipment you have freely chosen to take with you on this Lenten expedition.

Reflection

What can you as a member of a family, a household, a workplace or a community do with others as a Lenten activity, as a reminder that the journey of these Lenten days is a communal expedition? Do the Lenten works you have embraced have a communal dimension, or are they simply private and personal spiritual exercises?

Look back at page 12 of this mountain-climber's handbook and adjust or add to your self-imposed, freely chosen spiritual works for these forty days. Besides a commitment to the use of this guidebook, what other "special equipment" or allies can you select to help you choose life over death.

To reinforce that commitment to life, again challenge yourself to as much *secret* service, hidden kindness and underground prayer as possible. Beware of impressing others—or even yourself—with your spiritual allies.

Ash Friday

The prophet Isaiah implores us to fast today so as to make our voices heard on high (see Is. 58: 1-9).

John's disciples come to Jesus and ask why it is that they and the Pharisees fast while Jesus' disciples do not (see Mt. 9: 14-15).

Critical to any expedition is an adequate supply of food and water. Careful planning is required before an ascent to assure enough of these essential items. The paradox is that today is traditionally a day for a universal fast. While rightfully participating in this global religious act of fasting, reflect on what type of fasting you are called to practice as a disciple of Jesus.

The disciples of the ascetic John the Baptizer were shocked, as were the Pharisees, that Jesus and his disciples did not fast. Today's Gospel records the exchange in which Jesus compares himself to a bridegroom and calls into question all fasting that is a sign of mourning.

While fasting from food today, nibble on this parable-manuscript of the Lost Gospel of Matthew:

"Jesus, why do your disciples not fast?" asked a disciple of John.

"Ah, but we do," replied Jesus. "Only let those with eyes see."

Another disciple of John protested, "We see you and your followers eating and drinking, enjoying yourselves as at a feast!"

Jesus nodded. "Indeed, John's fasting is a holy work and

pleasing to God. It's a call to abstain as a sign of penance, a sign of mourning that the Messiah has not yet come. But look! The Messiah is here, among you, and he is a fasting Messiah!"

"If that is who you are, what kind of fast do you call this feasting?" John's disciples objected.

"The fast of Isaiah! The prophet has spoken for God, correct? Then it is only that kind of fast that God, the Blessed One, finds of interest!" Jesus continued to eat his dinner as he spoke.

Confused, they echoed, "Isaiah's fast?"

"Allow me to refer you to the scroll of the prophet Isaiah, chapter fifty-eight, where it says that the kind of fast God wishes is *releasing the bonds of those unjustly tied, setting free the oppressed, breaking every yoke, sharing your bread with the hungry, sheltering the oppressed and the homeless, clothing the naked and not turning your backs on your own.*"

Silence fell like frost on those around Jesus. He looked into the eyes of each of his questioners: "This is the fasting of the new reign of God that my disciples and I practice, not only on special days—as do you and the Pharisees—but on all days. This is the fasting that will make the Light blaze forth, that will truly bring about the coming of the Messiah."

Reflection

Ask yourself: Do I prefer to fast from food, to abstain from beef and chicken, since it's easier than struggling to create equality for everyone in my society? Do I use these holy days to diet for reasons of health and beauty—or as an occasion for a spiritual diet from what makes the world unhealthy and unholy?

Do I prefer to practice a spirituality that consents to society's blindness to the homeless? Do I choose a prayer-life whose sole intent is intimacy with God instead of including intimacy with those yoked by poverty and the myriad forms of institutional oppression?

Do I, together with fasting from food, care to select one or more of the forms of fasting proclaimed by the prophet and practiced by Jesus? Could I add one of those practices to my Lenten works?

20

Ash Saturday

The Prophet Isaiah says that if you remove oppression, false accusation and malicious speech from your midst, if you give your bread to the hungry and attend to the afflicted, then light will rise from you (see Is. 58: 9-14).

After Jesus calls Matthew the tax collector to follow him, the Pharisees and scribes ask Jesus why he eats with sinners and tax collectors. Jesus responds that only sick people need a doctor, that he has come not to invite the self-righteous to a change of heart, but sinners (see Lk. 5: 27-32).

Tomorrow we will begin the ascent of the Mountain of God. Today, our final day in base camp, take one last look at your willingness to go on this expedition. Indeed, the church—all churches—expect that everyone will embrace the rigors of the Lenten journey. In reality, some do and more do not.

This journey starts with a personal invitation: "Come, follow me," says Jesus. He says it to you as he said it to Matthew, who was busy at his office desk collecting toll taxes. Besides questioning his rejection of fasting, the Pharisees took delight in condemning Jesus for the company he kept—sinners and the outcasts of society. On this Easter expedition, while you might prefer to take saints as companions, Jesus selects a company composed of the sick of soul. While personally invited to follow him, do you qualify for companionship?

The purple of Lent is a good color to remind all of us that we are perpetual penitents, that we are sinners in the process of ongoing reform. As such, this Lenten journey of ascent reflects the entire Christian life. It's an upward path that requires more than an instant change of heart. The way of Jesus implies not just forty days but a continuous dropping of habits and behaviors that hold us back from ascending to God. Each Lent provides an opportunity for renewed commitment to a lifelong revolution within your heart, a spiritual evolution ever upward to greatness and holiness.

Isaiah reminds you, in case you've forgotten, that the proper work of Lent is not pious prayer—although that may be of assistance—but the work of removing oppression from your home, workplace and social environment.

You may have known the path of the old Lent—with its denial of pleasures, its stations of the cross, fast and abstinence—like the back of your hand. It would be natural to fear that if you venture forth on such a different, prophetic kind of Lent, you might lose your way. Fear not, Isaiah says, for God will be your compass if you follow God's way of fast and penance.

In the old Lent the various personal spiritual works were called Lenten penances. They were often harsh and heavy-handed acts of self-denial. Reflect today on how in the new Lent, which is taking shape because of the reforms inspired by the Holy Spirit in the Second Vatican Council, instead of penances we should select Lenten allies. The reflection for the Monday before Ash Wednesday advised you to travel lightly and wisely. It also suggested that you might wait till today before completing the selection of your allies.

These allies are whatever might assist or support your work toward the kind of inner reform that leads to the coming of the reign of God. As you form your list of allies, carefully choose three or four exercises, practices or spiritual works that will most assist your ascent of the Mountain of God. Be selective; limit your choices to those allies that you can stay with throughout the Lenten expedition and to those allies you need most right now to change your heart. As you prayerfully choose your allies, may the spirit of St. Isaiah be with you. As we prepare to leave the base camp tomorrow, remember: Travel lightly and wisely.

This expedition is ready to depart. Before you, looming tall and majestic is the sacred sierra of Lent. Between here and Mount Easter are the other peaks that are part of the mystic Lenten range. In your path, as well, are valleys, deserts, barren plateaus and rugged cliffs. Partially hidden by ominous clouds is the ugly specter of Mount Calvary. Before you lies the threat of rock or ice avalanches and various other dangers. And just ahead is the first foreboding mountain of the range which tomorrow you and Jesus shall climb.

Again, regardless of your age or physical condition, this will be a great adventure if you can give yourself to it with a fullness of heart and soul. Glorious will be this expedition experience if you embrace its call to holiness. Blessed are those eager to climb the Mountain of God.

And so, if after these days of preparation you still wish to continue, step forward. Show to Christ a sign of your desire to participate in this expedition—show your sickness to the Divine Healer!

Reflection

Since Jesus, as a healer of hearts, came to serve not the self-righteous but those in need of healing, what sickness or crippling soul-disease will you show to your Lord? This is not a pilgrimage for tourists or sightseers but for the sick.

Before you expose yourself to the divine physician, ask yourself: Do I really wish to be healed of this affliction of heart, soul or personality?

If after a personal examination you find nothing in need of healing, nothing in yourself that calls out to be changed or reformed, what should you do? Consider having the courage to ask a spouse, friend, partner or community member what he or she sees in you that needs healing.

Having completed the necessary work of preparation at base camp one, you can say in unison with all the other brave ones who have taken up this Lenten expedition, "Come, let us climb the Mountain of God!"

O God, come to my assistance. O Lord, make haste to help me as I take up my Lenten allies, and my cross, to climb your holy mountain.

First Sunday in Lent
Mount Diablo

Moses speaks of his peoples' freedom from slavery in Egypt (see Dt. 25: 4-10).

St. Luke describes how the devil took Jesus up a high mountain and tempted him, showing all the kingdoms of the world in a single instant (see Lk. 4: 1-13).

Just as the evil one took Jesus up a high mountain peak to tempt him, today you climb with Jesus up Mount Diablo! It is the peak that Jesus climbed as he began his forty days of soul-searching with God. It is the first mountain in the sacred sierra of the great Mountain of God. We will spend this next week traversing Mount Diablo, encountering different aspects of evil, exploring Jesus' way of remaining free from its slavery. As you ascend, pinned to your clothing or tied to your walking staff should be a blue ribbon, like the one that came with this manual, identifying you as a member of this Lenten expedition.

While purple is the traditional liturgical color of Lent, blue might be more appropriate, especially if we understand both the ongoing struggle of this season of personal reform and the conflict of today's first ascent up the awesome Mount Diablo, the Mount of the Devil. If heaven is where God is, then wherever you find the devil must be hell! If during these holy forty days you follow Jesus into the desert, then you too must journey into hell. And since you're going into combat with Satan, it's not the time for *the wearin' of the green*. It's the time for the wearin' of the blue.

Jesus and the people of his day didn't joke about devils and demons. They believed they were surrounded by swarms of diabolic spirits. These dark spirits caused all sorts of physical and social harm, sickness and confusion. Therefore, it was important to be protected by various charms and medallions and to know the proper incantations to ward off evil. Knowing how to use herbal protections like garlic and onions was equally essential to them.

The classical protection for Christians is holy water. For centuries, the official night prayer of the church included the admonition of St. Peter to *stay sober and alert, for our enemy, the devil, is prowling like a roaring lion looking for someone to devour. We are to resist him, solid in our faith* (see 1 Pt. 5:8). In houses of religious communities, the superior would sprinkle members with holy water at this night prayer to guard them against the lurking devil. This custom of sprinkling one's bed at nightfall was also a custom in the homes of the faithful to ward off the prowling lion of evil.

This first Sunday in Lent recounts Jesus' encounter with that prowling mountain lion. St. Luke didn't say whether Jesus was wearing anything blue, but that color was prominent in the ancient world as a safeguard against demons and evil. Doors and window frames of homes were painted blue. Men as well as women used blue eye shadow, particularly in ancient Egypt, not for beauty but for protection. Blue ribbons or blue articles of clothing were worn as a defense—that's the reason why baby boys traditionally have been dressed in blue: to protect them from the devil. (You might ask, "Well, what does pink protect girls from?" The answer is: "Nothing!" While that may sound shocking, the color pink for girls was introduced no more than a hundred years ago by the clothing industry simply to sell clothing for baby girls!)

Blue, then, is the great antidote color for evil, and it's also a good, vibrant color to awaken you to the new Lent. Some still prefer to celebrate the old Lent of purple penance and denial. Your blue ribbon can remind you not to be tempted to return to the practices of the old Lent just because they are familiar and therefore comfortable. The penitential nature of the old Lent had its roots in a literary accident by St. Jerome, who transcribed the Scriptures from Greek into Latin. He mistranslated the words of Jesus about preparing for the reign of God as, "*Do penance*, the kingdom of God is at hand."

Doing penance as a Lenten directive has meant giving up sweets, abstaining from things you enjoy, fasting, denying yourself, and even wearing a hair shirt. But ask yourself the question: How does that type of behavior bring about the Kingdom? Does the reign of God come about by wearing a penitential hair shirt or giving up sweets? Purple penance has a legitimate place as a response to having sinned, but in today's watered-down version of Lent or as the primary direction of this season, it can easily miss the mark.

From where you stand atop Mount Diablo, look out across the hogbacks—those sharp, rough ridges with steeply sloping sides that give shape to the days of this first week of Lent. As you scan the horizon for what lies ahead, ask yourself: Lest I miss the mark, what is the real purpose of Lent?

Reflection

Hold your blue Lenten bookmark and ask yourself: Can I be tempted to spend this Lent as an overprotected, pious personal exercise in spiritual growth—and so fail to bring about the reign of God in myself and in my world?

Reflect on the three tests given Jesus by the evil one. Ask yourself what three tests you might find most difficult to endure and consider what allies Jesus might help you to choose in confronting these tests. If you were to face such a test this day, perhaps it would be a good idea to carry your blue ribbon in your pocket.

This first Sunday in Lent is a good time to again reexamine your Lenten practices, the list of allies you have chosen for your mountain-climbing expedition, to ensure that they are the ones God most desires.

First Monday in Lent

God tells Moses to tell the whole Israelite community to be holy, for God is holy (see Lv. 19: 1-2, 11-18).

At the final judgment, Jesus tells his sheep that they are to receive God's blessing and inherit the kingdom because they gave him food when he was hungry and drink when he was thirsty (see Mt. 25: 31-46).

Today you are given the goal of your ascent up the Mountain of God: to become godlike, to be holy as God is holy. The new Lent provides you with a new direction toward holiness that is evident in the new translation, a more correct translation, of the original Greek. Jesus' call isn't to "do penance" but to "reform your life." Reform, reshaping, involves much more than doing penance. Reform is not redecoration but radical reconstruction! Perhaps we could start this Lenten expedition with a trinity of colors as sacred signposts. The purple of penance could remind us of the original meaning of sin: to miss the mark. It could call us to a willingness to radically change our ways so that something truly new might be born.

The season of Lent and our communal ascent up the Mountain of God begins in the cold chill of winter, in the bleak highlands of the winter season of cold grays and lifeless browns. Day-by-day as our Lenten expedition unfolds, green creeps across the landscape of Earth's northern hemisphere. Slowly, as we make our ascent to Easter, lawns, trees and fields begin to turn green with the coming of spring. Green is the color of new birth, the color of transformation from death and drab winter to the new life of spring. Green, then, can be the Lenten color that symbolizes the new direction of this season.

Blue, to ward off evil, can be the color of those Lenten works that free us from any form of slavery to evil. Blue can serve to protect us from small compromises with evil that lead to larger capitulations. Blue can be the color of exercises of reform that liberate you and the world from secret little deals with the devil.

With the approach of spring, besides the song of birds, the sound of frogs will be heard. In early Christianity, frogs were believed to be signs of the devil! Their raucous croaking was compared to the sound of heretics spreading their evils. As we pass over Mount Diablo and along the ridge into this first week of Lent, it's wise to be aware of the presence of evil on this journey. Sunday's Gospel is a reminder: when the devil had finished tempting Jesus in the desert, he departed from him "for a time," to await another opportunity. When you hear the sound of croaking frogs, let your ever present blue-ribbon bookmark remind you to ward off the advances of evil.

Perhaps this week's Scripture passages and these reflections on the devil will challenge what you believe about evil. G.K. Chesterton tells us that when God departs, half-gods arrive. Our world too easily embraces half-gods in its worship of power, greed and other dark energies. While you may disbelieve in the devil, would you say that our world is free of evil? The twentieth century has seen an abundance of both global and local wars, with indiscriminate destruction and the killing of civilians. The American Civil War general, William T. Sherman, said, "It is only those who have neither fired a shot or heard the shrieks and groans of the wounded who cry aloud for blood, more vengeance, more desolation. War is hell!" If war is hell, then truly diabolic has been this century! Consider Hitler's concentration camps and his annihilation of over six million Jews, as well as homosexuals, gypsies and other "undesirables." Can you doubt the reality of evil in a century of sadistic torture of political prisoners, the exploitation of the poor in the third world, racial and religious discrimination, child and spousal abuse and growing social violence? Can the destructive environmental abuse of our planet—its air, water and soil—in the name of greed and apathy be anything but evil?

Serious reflection on these and other forms of corporate evil in our world reinforces how the purple of Lent is still a very appropriate color for our world, our nation, the church and for you and me as individuals. All individuals share in their nation's and the world's sins, so to various degrees you and I each share that guilt.

Reflection

You will be tempted, not only on this Lenten Monday but day in and day out, to compromise your principles when faced with evil. May you be protected from the sin of a lip-sealed silence in the face of social evils. May you be protected from looking the other way when injustice is at work.

In today's Gospel parable about the sheep and the goats, Jesus judges those blind to his presence in the poor, imprisoned and oppressed to be worthy of eternal punishment. As you read this chapter of the Gospel, look in the mirror and honestly ask yourself how you may be living as a goat.

O God, come to my assistance. O Lord, make haste to help me as I take up my Lenten allies, and my cross, to climb your holy mountain.

First Tuesday in Lent

Isaiah tells us that God's word, like fertile rain, is always fruitful and always achieves its end (see Is. 55: 10-11).

Jesus advises us to pray that we won't be subjected to the trial and that we might be delivered from the evil one (see Mt. 6: 7-15).

The beautiful passage from Isaiah once again calls into question the very existence of evil. After all, if God's word is always fruitful, what real power can evil have? On the other hand, why would Jesus, *the* Word, give us the famous prayer for deliverance from the evil one?

How you respond to the reality of evil may depend on whether you're a man or a woman. According to various polls, slightly more women, 58%, than men, 53%, believe in the devil. If you are a Protestant, you are more likely to believe in the devil than if you are a Roman Catholic: 62% compared to 51%. And 75% of born-again, fundamentalist Christians believe in the devil!

So, fellow mountain climber, as we make our way along the hogback ridge of Mount Diablo, when it comes to the existence of the evil one, what do you think? Is it a myth, a religious legend, or a reality?

As you reflect on the experience of Jesus with the devil, you may find it interesting that in a recent Gallup survey 10% of Americans reported having the very same experience. As with Jesus on Mount Diablo, the devil spoke to them and they to the devil. As an educated Christian you may dismiss with a smile such reports about Satan—that is, until you're informed that a satanic cult has moved in next door to you!

Some of us may question the reality of the devil. But, again, none of us question the existence of evil. And faced with myriad social and personal evils, you may be tempted to adopt the stance of the famous three monkeys: see, hear and speak no evil! The nightly content of the network news is hard stuff. Like the devil tempting Jesus in the desert, it's tempting to try to make the hard rocks of reality into bread—soft pious bread—which we may stick in our ears so that we hear no evil. It's easy to be blind and deaf to evil, to refrain from rocking the boat or blowing the whistle. It's easier to genuflect to evil so as not to be unpopular or lose your job.

Unlike Jesus, our encounters with evil are usually so domestic. It's easy to strike a little deal with darkness, especially when you've got two or three mouths to feed, or when getting involved might be unpleasant or even dangerous. Perhaps part of your creed is: Don't get involved if it's none of your business. However, not cooperating with evil requires great courage. There's an old expression that the road to hell is paved with good intentions; the road to hell is also downhill and easy.

In today's Gospel, Jesus tells his disciples how to pray. He offers what has become our most common prayer, the *Lord's Prayer*. Mindful of the ongoing challenge—and of our fears—in dealing with evil, the conclusion of Jesus' prayer directly asks for deliverance from the evil one.

Prayer and Reflection

Deliver me from the evil of sealed lips, I pray, O God,
  whenever I'm tempted to not speak out
  when others are unjustly treated or abused.
Deliver me from spiritual myopia, the evil of nearsighted eyes,
  when my concerns for the safety and welfare of others
  are restricted only to those who are closest to me.

Today's question for reflection: Does my failure to cultivate a daily discipline of good prayer make me easy prey to evil?

First Wednesday in Lent

God sends the prophet Jonah to the great city of Nineveh to announce that in forty days it will be destroyed. The people believe God's warning and proclaim a fast (see Jon. 3: 1-10).

Jesus tells the crowd that they live in an evil age that needs a sign. Jesus, however, gives it no sign except the sign of Jonah (see Lk. 11: 29-32).

On this Lenten Wednesday, our reflection is the story of the reluctant prophet Jonah, who was sent to reform the evil city of Nineveh in an evil age. Jesus too told the crowd that they lived in an evil age, that they looked only for special signs. How accurately that also applies to our age, in which the call to reformation is silenced by those who do not want to see any change in the evils in our present system.

The evil one did not tempt Jesus with lust, gambling, drug abuse or drunkenness, but with something much more subtle. Similarly, the evil in our age is not merely an expression of isolated and external sins. The temptation to lust is more a symptom of the disease. The roots of the disease lie intertwined with the roots of capitalism, the free market system. Its creed so easily is translated as, "I will get as much as I can from you and give you in return as little as possible. If I can do it, I will give you nothing, while trying to get everything from you."

Unlike Jesus' first disciples, who were politically powerless, we are disciples who have power, the great power of the ballot. Since it is a powerful tool, the evil one will be active when you want to use it. The voting booth may not appear to be a place where the devil will put you to the test. Yet, the first temptation is "Why bother? You know the political system isn't going to really change. So, stay home, save yourself the effort—don't vote."

If you do vote, be cautious as you go to the polls—wear your blue ribbon. As you enter the voting booth, evil will be lurking there tempting you to compromise in various ways. The prime temptation will be greed. "No new taxes!" is still a popular slogan, and probably always will be. That slogan can also read, "No new schools. No proper salaries for teachers or funds for new equipment. No homes for the homeless or jobs for the jobless. No care for the sick who are poor or for the elderly. No cleanup for the environment." The temptation of "no new taxes" is one of greed, since it allows you to keep more money in your pocket.

Also, wear or take your blue ribbon when you go into work. For at work you are prone to "innocent" evil: taking paper clips, getting as much out of the boss as possible while putting in a minimum of time and energy. Greed and exploitation can work in both directions at the workplace.

Wear the blue ribbon at home too because that's where you're most likely to hear dark voices tempting you to pout, to get revenge, to return injury for injury. Those voices will tell you that you have a "right" to be angry, that you're "justified" in throwing someone out of your heart.

In this sacred season of prayer and spiritual works, wear or take your blue ribbon whenever you go to pray! When Jesus went to pray in the desert, the devil came to visit. So hold your ribbon when you pray, because the devil is right there on the face of the clock that says, "There's no time. You're too busy to pray! It's too barren in this desert of prayer. Leave this silent time and place—go do something productive."

32

Reflection

The Hebrew word for temptation means "to test." Lent is a time to examine how your principles are tested in the reality of this hectic age in which we live. Ask yourself if you can pass the *apathy vs. social concern* test or the *greed vs. social concern* test.

You are also tested by time. Reflecting on the face of your clock as a face of evil can be a good exercise in determining how time tests your behavior. Ask yourself: Because the hands of the clock are moving too quickly, have I failed to take time to listen to others with full attention?

The English philosopher Francis Bacon (1561-1626) wrote in an essay, "If one be gracious and courteous to strangers, it shows you are a citizen of the world." Have you, because of the pressure of the clock, excused yourself from the prayer of kindness to strangers and so betrayed your real citizenship?

The next time the face of your clock or watch tempts you to be non-prayerful or disrespectful, may you look closely at it to see exactly whose face it is.

O God, come to my assistance. O Lord, make haste to help me as I take up my Lenten allies, and my cross, to climb your holy mountain.

First Thursday in Lent

Esther prays for the protective power of God because she is alone except for the divine presence. She asks God to put in her mouth persuasive words in the face of the lion (see Est. C: 12, 14-16, 23-25).

Jesus tells us that if we ask, we will receive; that if we seek, we will find (see Mt. 7: 7-12).

In this expedition of reform and renewal, each of the forty days is like a journey of forty miles—of forty very long steps. It is only natural that you might look for something convenient, like an escalator or a chairlift, to take you to the summit of Mount Easter. Prayerfully hold your blue ribbon and realize that there's no easy way to reach the top of the mountain. Be aware that each step you attempt to skip or sidestep will come up again and again until you find the courage to face it directly.

Whenever you are tested, let the blue of your ribbon remind you of the blue sky, the heavenly umbrella overhead. Just as Jesus was protected in the desert by God's Spirit, so you also are under God's care. As Job and Abraham were tested in their loyalty to God, so you too will be tested, but take heart—as Jesus was strengthened in his desert test, you also will be empowered by God. Pray Esther's prayer of poverty, which asked God for help because she was alone and had no one but God. You can add to her prayer that you *need* no one other than God.

Today's good news is Jesus' affirmation that if you ask, you will receive; if you seek, you will find. He also taught that God knows your every daily need, so pray for what you really need— gifts of the spirit, a flaming zeal, meekness of heart.

Recalling his *prayer of prayers*, pray especially to be protected from the evil one. You can pray that prayer with confidence since, ultimately, goodness will triumph over evil as long as enough of us refuse to cooperate or compromise with evil.

In every aspect of your daily life you will be tested, even— and, perhaps, especially—in church! Wear your blue ribbon or carry it in your pocket when you go to church because the devil, like a roaring lion, loves to lurk in liturgies and holy places. Indeed, Jesus went into the desert to be with God, yet the devil was also there! As you sit listening to a sermon about social justice, be on your guard if in your inner ear you hear a little voice croaking that there should be separation between church and state. Clever is the voice that whispers, "Keep politics and social issues out of religion!"

You also surrender to the power of evil whenever you mentally curl up in the fetal position and do nothing, saying to yourself, "Let the experts take care of this injustice. Let the people with briefcases, the authorities and experts in politics, religion and world reform attend to it. It's none of my business—besides, it's beyond my means."

Find hope in the flag of our expedition which is a rainbow-colored flag. At its top is a broad band of purple as a reminder to atone for both personal and corporate sins. Corporate, you ask? Have not one hundred percent of us cooperated with evil in some way, made our own secret little deals? Below the purple is a band of green which symbolizes a sign of hope that together we can turn things around, that a true reconstruction of hearts is possible. The blue on the expedition's flag proclaims that even though evil is extremely powerful and will test us again and again, we are under God's care and protection. Next on the flag is a band of yellow. As the sign of a coward, yellow cautions us to be on guard not to betray Christ or our mission because of fearing to stand up for what we know is true. Yellow is also a warm color, a sign of the sun, and it can remind us not to be lukewarm in our Lenten devotion. Recall the words of Christ in the book of Revelation about wishing we were either hot or cold, and spewing the lukewarm out of his mouth (see Rev. 3: 15-16). Finally, our Lenten flag has a band of red for sacrifice and love, both of which are essential for anyone seeking to reach the summit of the Mountain of God.

Each time you pray the Lord's Prayer, as you approach the end, pray slowly: "Lead us not into the trial, into temptation, but deliver us from evil." Be aware that the test may not involve being a fanatic—too hot—or rejecting God—too cold—but rather being lukewarm. The real temptation might be betraying the Gospel for the sake of convenience or out of fear of shame. Every time you pray that prayer of Jesus, acknowledge that evil exists. Pray with confidence that you, like Jesus, will be delivered and not be defeated by evil. Trust that God's word indeed will bear fruit in your life.

Reflection

The goal of our ascent is holiness. The first letter of Peter recalls the purpose of these Lenten days: it says that you are to *become holy yourself in every aspect of your conduct, in the pattern of the Holy One who called you.* You need to remember, how *you are called to be holy as God is holy* (see 1 Pt. 1: 15).

That letter of Peter also affirms the dignity of our ragtag company climbing this Mountain of God. We may be a company of sinners and the spiritually sick, but we are a priestly expedition. The second chapter sings out the good news that *we are living stones, built as a structure of the Spirit*; we are *a holy priesthood*— we have the power *to offer spiritual sacrifices acceptable to God* (see 1 Pt. 2: 5).

As a priest of the new reign of God, ask yourself how you can live a life in which you are both the gift-victim and the priest who offers the gift to God.

Is the goal of holiness one of your great desires in life?

First Friday in Lent

The prophet Ezekiel proclaims God's message that if sinners turn away from sin and follow God's statutes they will come to life (see Ez. 18: 21-28).

Jesus advises us that unless our holiness surpasses that of the scribes and Pharisees we will not enter the kingdom of God (see Mt. 5: 20-26).

Traveling the hogback ridge of Mount Diablo, these words of Jesus are a warning that not everyone will reach the ultimate summit! Recall the reflection earlier in this first Lenten week on the challenge God gave to Moses and the people about being holy as God is holy. Jesus clarified that challenge when he calls us to a holiness *greater* than one that can be gained merely by following the law.

For most of us, holiness seems to be a destination that's out of reach. Only saints are holy, and how many saints do you know on a first-name basis? Being good is a more realistic goal. Yet

Jesus called each of us to a holiness which surpasses that of the acknowledged law-abiding perfectionists of his day! The Pharisees and the scribes (the original lay ministers), were zealous in keeping even the most minute religious legalisms. How then can you or I scale the towering heights of holiness?

A true story from the history of Australia will be a backpack parable for exploring Jesus' challenge to rise to greater heights of holiness than even the pious law-keepers could attain. Australia, as a pioneer land, was first settled by prisoners from England. Present-day Sydney was England's first penal colony where convicts were sent to be isolated from the rest of humanity. Having served their prison sentences, and lacking the means to return to England, the released prisoners found themselves trapped in the desolate wasteland of Australia.

The governor of the colony realized not only that the land needed to be developed but also that there were many willing and eager to try to tame the land. The ocean bounded the territory on the east, with a great range of mountains on the western border, while to the north and south were swamps and deserts. In the late eighteenth and early nineteenth centuries, expeditions were sent to cross over the mountains toward the interior of the continent. Yet each one failed. Finally, the leaders of the government declared defeat in the effort to seek expansion to the west, and the mountain range was named the Barrier Mountains.

In 1812, however, three daring young men set out on an expedition to conquer the Barrier Mountains. Having studied the routes and efforts of the previous, failed expeditions, the three decided upon a different approach when they came to the area of the most difficult cliffs. They planned on using only the hardest routes. They outfitted their expedition with twice as many horses, foodstuffs, supplies and men as they felt were needed. People made fun of them and of their desire to cross the insurmountable Barrier Mountains. When asked why they were taking so many supplies, they responded, "Because we will need them to settle the land once we are on the other side."

They stayed away from the easy valleys and took the hard route, the difficult way avoided by other explorers. First they climbed the hills, the lower ridges which led to the more difficult mountain peaks that lay ahead. Finally, by following the top of the ridge they reached the highest peak and named it Mount York. Beyond that peak, they could see rolling valleys and a land rich with forests. There they settled and began the expansion of Australia.

Reflection

This parable-story is a compass confirmation for the Lenten expedition. Becoming holy is for the majority of people like the Barrier Mountains: an impossible destination! Indeed, if you choose an easy, convenient path, which emphasizes external laws and practices rather than real inner reform, you will find barrier after barrier to holiness. Recall the words of Jesus on Ash Thursday that all those who wish to follow him must deny themselves, take up their crosses and climb in his footsteps.

Be willing to embrace the struggle and hard work of self-denial and sacrificial living if you wish to reach the summit of life, holiness. This expedition called Lent is not an ascent of forty days in which you simply climb the mountain, plant the flag, and then return to your former life. Like the victorious team that scaled Australia's Barrier Mountains, in this expedition the plan is to settle and explore on the other side!

You have departed for a new place, a new way to live, where the reforms of the ascent you've embraced with love will become an integrated part of your lifestyle. Any other intention for this pilgrimage to the Mountain of God is a waste of time! If you don't seek to settle on the other side, this expedition will be only forty pious days of religious fervor, which soon after the Easter sun has risen will wither and die.

O God, come to my assistance. O Lord, make haste to help me as I take up my Lenten allies, and my cross, to climb your holy mountain.

First Saturday in Lent

Moses talks to the people about God's covenant with them: they are to be faithful to God's commands with their whole heart and soul, and God will make them a sacred people (see Dt. 26: 16-19).

Jesus says that we need to do more than just love those who love us, that we must be perfect as God is perfect (see Mt. 5: 43-48).

Your Lenten expedition's blue ribbon can become your *cordon bleu*. That term is usually associated with a restaurant's preparation of chicken or veal combined with ham, melted cheese and a white sauce. The term originated not with chicken but with Edward III of England. About a hundred and fifty years before Columbus, King Edward attended a ball and was dancing with the Princess of Salisbury when her blue garter slipped and fell to the floor. Amidst the laughter of those at the ball, Edward calmly picked up the garter and handed it back to her. He said to the snickering crowd, "*Honi soit qui mal y pense* (Shame to the one who thinks evil of it)."

Edward III then instituted the Order of the Cordon Bleu (the blue garter) in 1344 and had symbolic garters inscribed with his words about those who think evil. It became a universally coveted badge of honor. Under the Bourbons in France the *cordon bleu* was the symbol of the highest order of knighthood. Later it was used to honor great chefs, and finally was given to dishes of outstanding quality. The blue ribbon, from county fairs to sports awards, became the award of excellence.

In England, the blue garter of the Order of St. George became the most distinguished award of the realm, being worn on the left leg just below the knee. Perhaps a blue garter should be placed on Jesus' left leg in figures of his crucifixion! To Jesus belongs the highest award for courage and for not compromising with evil. If, like him, you can ascend the forty steps of Lent, traveling with fidelity each of the forty days, climbing ever higher and higher, you will finally come to the summit, to the perfection of holiness to which you are called. If you have the strength to continue this expedition as a faithful mountaineer, then on Easter Sunday morning on the lapel of your suit or on your Easter bonnet, you too with pride can wear the *cordon bleu.*

Having traveled during these past days along the rough, jagged ridge of Mount Diablo, we are now prepared to climb to the next peak, Mount Tabor. There, at the next level of the sacred sierras, a vision-experience that is a preview to Easter awaits you.

Reflection

Frequently, when presented with some great challenge that tests your willingness for self-sacrifice, a little dark voice can whisper, "Why burn yourself out for those who don't appreciate what you're doing for them? What difference will your sacrifice or efforts make in the long run?"

The challenge of greatness—whether spiritual, athletic, intellectual or artistic—is found in the universal call to heroism. Lent calls for heroines and heroes willing to deny themselves to attain God's kind of perfection—to make their world more beautiful, more just and more loving. No single action of heroic sacrifice is ever wasted or goes unnoticed.

In the Theater of Destiny, where only God, the angels and saints watch the performance, each of us is called to faithfully act out our part in the Drama. Each of us is first required to know, and then embrace, our unique part in the Divine Comedy. If you can accept your part and have the courage to fulfill your destiny, rejoice. For at the great cosmic curtain call, to the thundering roar of the heavenly crowd, you will be awarded the eternal cordon bleu!

Second Sunday in Lent
Mount Tabor

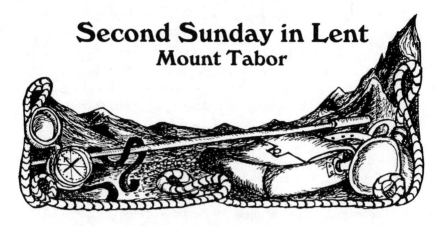

God makes a covenant with Abraham and with his countless descendants (see Gn. 15: 5-12, 17-18).

We hear how Jesus took Peter, John and James up a mountain to pray (see Lk. 9: 28-36).

Having traveled one week along the hogback ridge from Mount Diablo, we have climbed a higher peak to open this second week of Lent. This new mountain has traditionally been called Mount Tabor. It is the site of the Transfiguration.

Jesus and his friends went up on a mountain to pray. It's a scene that echoes a long spiritual legacy. Throughout the ages a mountain has been God's chosen secret meeting place. In God's rendezvous on Mount Sinai with Moses, they spoke as friends, and God gave to Moses the Law. It was on Mount Moriah that Abraham was tested as he took his beloved son to be slaughtered as an offering to God, to *El Shaddai*, as Abraham called the God of his family—*El* meaning "God" and *Shaddai*, "Almighty." Some have suggested that a more precise translation of *El Shaddai* would be "the One of the Mountain." This Lenten expedition is a journey to the One of the Mountain, reflecting Jesus' journey up to Jerusalem. The path will eventually take you to another mountain, Mount Calvary, where Jesus would have his final earthly rendezvous with God.

Today's mountain experience foreshadows Mount Easter and the glory that would be Christ's after passing through the shame and the disgrace of the cross. The vision on Mount Tabor has Jesus visiting with two holy prophets, Moses and Elijah, as he is transformed, transfigured, in dazzling white garments. The actual clothing of Jesus as a peasant craftsman would have been a drab brown-gray, but on the mountain his robes became whiter than any bleach could make them. On that day of the transfiguration, God was the washer-woman, but soon Jesus would do his own laundry.

Today also gives a glimpse of the glory of your own transfiguration if you remain faithful in doing your laundry. Besides being essential Lenten work, it's appropriate that doing the laundry has become a much more universal image in contemporary culture. Once seen only as woman's work, today both men and women go about that weekly duty, whether at home or at the laundromat.

Before we explore the implications of a laundry spirituality, however, let us take time to examine the heavenly visitors who were with Jesus. What if the vision were recast with symbols more relevant to our age? Picture, for a moment, Jesus dressed in blood-red garments, with Lenin and George Washington standing on his left and right. What? Two revolutionaries? That scenario may sound strange, but consider for a moment that while Moses and Elijah were prophets, they were also political rebels. Moses rebelled against the entire Egyptian empire in history's first great revolution of little and powerless people. Elijah spoke boldly to King Ahab, telling him that he was a fool to trust in his armies and weapons, for only God could be his salvation and the hope of his people. For Elijah that rebellious stance was costly; he, like Moses, was hunted down by his government as a rebel.

Standing between these two fugitives, Jesus is dressed in white—interestingly white, and not red, is Christianity's color of martyrdom! It was the color, for the first audience of the Gospel, of the early Christian martyrs. Recall in the book of Revelation how there appeared a vast throng dressed in long white robes, holding palm branches in their hands. They were *the ones who had survived the great period of trial and had washed their robes, making them white in the blood of the Lamb* (see Rev. 7: 9-14).

So Jesus appeared not just in glory but also as a martyr in this mountaintop vision. As a martyr he was not just crucified, he was *executed* by the empire and the temple. As is usually the case, the executioners' accomplices were the docile and silent masses who bowed before the power of those two mighty institutions.

Yet as a rebel and martyr, Jesus was unique. Although his cause of justice was radically revolutionary, he accomplished it without violence. While he was charged with sedition against the empire and sacred sedition against the temple, he was actually murdered in the name of peace and love.

Reflection

While in all probability you will not actually be called to offer up your life for the cause of peace and love, what are you willing to give up for them? Are you willing to look the fool for love? Are you willing to appear weak for the sake of peace—and so be transformed?

Today, reflect on your fidelity to your allies on this expedition called Lent. Turn back to page 12 and reread them. Examine if you have been faithful to them not out of discipline but because of great love.

Second Monday in Lent

Daniel assures us that the great and awesome God has a merciful way toward those who love God and observe God's commandments (see Dn. 9: 4-10).

Jesus tells us to be compassionate as God is compassionate (see Lk. 6: 36-38).

Awesome to his three disciples was the vision of the village craftsman, Jesus, transformed by God's glory on Mount Tabor. Today we continue to reflect on the meaning of his transfiguration. While condemned as a rebel and executed between two criminals, never did Jesus by word or action promote armed rebellion or violence against either the empire or the religious establishment. He taught his followers never to return injury for injury, never to take up the sword—for those who live by the sword will die by it.

His followers were called to resist evil—but to do so in a nonviolent way, regardless of whether the oppressor was the empire or a neighbor. The revolution of Jesus confronted the disease of evil at its breeding ground in the heart. The enormous depth of his revolution is felt in his powerful words that even to become angry with another is to be guilty of murder! Today, as in Jesus' time, such an uprising as the Revolt of the Dove is thought to be folly and filled with madness.

To better understand the Gospel's revolutionary message and its secret power, let's again switch the visitors at the site of the Transfiguration. Instead of Moses and Elijah, place Gandhi, the nonviolent leader of India, on one side of Jesus, and Tolstoy, the Russian author and peacemaker, on the other. Listen in on their imagined conversation as Jesus says, "I know what I have heard from God. I know what I've heard whispered in the ear of my heart: that I am to remove the oppression in my peoples' lives. But I am to do it not by war, armed sedition or violence. Yet many look for me to overthrow the empire with force, and even my companions say to me, 'There is no other way!'"

Gandhi replies, "The state's evil is not the cause but the effect of social evil. The only way of curing the disease is by removing the cause thereof: let the people purify themselves."

Tolstoy nods in agreement and adds, "Human life is better ensured by the law of love than the law of violence. The law of violence is the most horrible of all mistakes."

Those are direct quotes from the teachings of Gandhi and Tolstoy. They help us understand the teaching of Jesus to his disciples, including you and me. The word *martyr* is Greek for "witness." If you witness in your daily life to the law of love and compassion, you will bring peace to your world, you will change and heal the whole world. To live out such a teaching is to choose a daily martyrdom of nonviolence—defenseless, yet refusing to be intimidated by or to cooperate with the power of evil. It's a commitment to the painful struggle of never letting the disease of anger or resentment—which is old anger—take root in your heart.

Reflection

The famous bank robber, John Dillinger, and his gang held up the Central National Bank of Greencastle, Indiana. It was their largest robbery, netting them $75,346. In the midst of the holdup, an elderly foreign-born woman, unruffled by the situation, started out the back door of the bank. The member of the gang posted at the door gently told her, "Better go back inside, lady." She brushed aside his gun and snapped, in her heavy accent, "I go to Penneys! And you go to hell!" She walked out of the bank and down the street unharmed.

To be a nonviolent witness who resists evil requires courage and commitment. God, the Awesome One, protects those who are faithful to the covenant and who love God.

Try to anticipate how you might react the next time you are tested in an encounter with evil. Could you, like the elderly immigrant lady, tell evil to go home and leave you alone?

O God, come to my assistance. O Lord, make haste to help me as I take up my Lenten allies, and my cross, to climb your holy mountain.

Second Tuesday in Lent

Isaiah gives us God's message to wash ourselves clean, to put away our misdeeds from before God's eyes, to cease doing evil and learn to do good. We are to make justice our aim (see Is. 1: 10, 16-20).

Jesus advises us that the greatest among us will be those who serve the rest (see Mt. 23: 1-12).

As you, along with the rest of our Lenten expedition, descend from Mount Tabor into the saddle, the lowest point between this and the next summit, it's time for cleansing. A small stream flows here in this desert area, and following Isaiah's advice, we're encouraged to pause and wash up. Cleanliness is the enemy of all disease. The evil of the empire and the establishment is as contagious today as it has always been. Yet it is not the cause, as Gandhi said, but the effect of the disease.

Violence, as with any infectious disease—like AIDS, for example—is something that children can be exposed to even in the womb. They absorb violence in their homes, they pick it up in school, and they spread the virus to others as they grow older. The good news is that the disease can be cured by doing your laundry! Recall Gandhi's wise words, "Let the people purify themselves." More than purifying or washing your clothing, what is needed is a frequent, even daily, washing of your words, thoughts and life in the blood of the Lamb.

A good contemporary symbol for this Lenten work would be a box of laundry soap or a plastic jug of bleach. You might place these common laundry-room items in your prayer corner this week. They can be secular-sacred symbols to remind you to do your laundry each night, to purify yourself, to bleach out the stains of anger and resentment. Jesus called us to such nightly laundry when he told us to never let the sun set on our anger.

In his spiritual classic, *The Ascent of Mount Carmel*, St. John of the Cross said, "When the patriarch Jacob desired to ascend Mount Bethel to build an altar for offering sacrifice to God, he first ordered his people to do three things: to destroy all strange gods; to purify themselves; and to change their garments. Those desiring to climb the summit of the mount in order to become an altar for the offering of a sacrifice of pure love and praise and reverence to God must first accomplish these three tasks."

Several weeks after Harry Truman was elected president, the head of the White House servants came to him. Nervously he said, "Mr. President, we have a problem. In doing the White House laundry, we seem to have misplaced your underwear and socks!" President Truman smiled. "You didn't lose them. I wash my own underwear and my own socks."

Shocked, the White House servant replied, "But, sir, why

would you want to wash your own underwear and socks?" The president said, "My mother taught me to do that when I left home to get married. She said, 'Harry, never let your wife do your personal laundry. You do it yourself.'" And so he did, even while president of the United States. Washing your underwear—and washing feet—can be powerful bleachers of pride for anyone.

Reflection

You too must do your personal dirty laundry, your Lenten laundry. In the blood of the Lamb, risen and glorious, cleanse yourself of injustice, violence and any other stains of evil you find within yourself.

St. Isaiah's advice that we learn to do good is an invitation to make this Lenten expedition not only an ascent up the mountain of God but also a traveling school of saints. What *new* kind of good are you willing to learn to do today?

Second Wednesday in Lent

The citizens of Jerusalem plot against Jeremiah, who asks God if good must be repaid with evil (see Jer. 18: 18-20).

Jesus takes the apostles aside and tells them that they are about to go up to Jerusalem, where the Son of Man will be handed over to the chief priests and scribes and condemned to death. Jesus adds that anyone who aspires to greatness must serve the rest, must serve the needs of all (see Mt. 20: 17-28).

Midweek, our expedition must continue to climb upward again toward Jerusalem and Mount Calvary. But before you reach the summit, Mount Horeb-Sinai (scholars believe that Horeb and Sinai are names for the same holy mountain) blocks the view. And before you depart from the streambed where you've paused in the desert, make sure that you have done the laundry.

Doing the laundry can just be a nuisance, an unpleasant task. Lent, however, calls you to the laundry of prayer, real prayer, where God's cleansing light is allowed into the hidden corners of your heart. Lent calls you to silent sitting, to prayerful meditation, to quietly observing your thoughts. Meditation illuminates what is often unconscious and points out what must be laundered. Silence is a strong bleach! In addition, the secret service of Lent, hidden deeds of charity and kindness, can effectively cleanse your desires for fame, attention or self-gratification and so make your deeds pure and transfigured.

Today in our health-conscious society, we are told to keep careful watch over our hearts. Like many of us, you may be concerned about the amount of fat in your diet and your level of cholesterol. It's even more a matter of life and death that you be concerned about the amount of anger and ill-will that clogs your heart. Whenever you feel you have been the victim of an injury—a nasty word or some slight, slander or rude remark—cleanse yourself by blessing with love the person responsible. It may not be easy to have unconditional positive regard for an "enemy." At first you might try to find one good thing you could wish for that person. If, at least in some small way, you can pray daily for your enemies, for those who misunderstand you, you will truly have a healthy heart.

If you find yourself in an argument, don't try to win it—at least to win it by using the conventional weapons of physical or verbal violence, or any power or authority you might possess. Instead, wash the exchange with love and compassion. Seek in your interpersonal differences a consensus, which is not just some middle ground, but a real consensus: *con-sentire*, to "feel with" the other.

A true resolution of difficulties comes from feeling what the other feels, desiring a one-mindedness, a one-heartedness. Such a holy state serves the needs of others. It's the kind of service to which Jesus in today's Gospel called you and all his disciples. If the cycle of violence and war, the cycle of sickness seen nightly in the news, is ever to end, the cure must begin in your heart, home and workplace.

Resist the ever abiding temptation to believe that making more laws will accomplish the coming of an age of peace and justice. As with the Pharisees and scribes, laws will never prevent war and hate or promote love and peace. Even the best diplomatic efforts of the world's nations cannot outlaw war. Jesus did not believe in a code of laws. He knew the road to the reign of God was not paved with laws, since laws are often only a subtle form of violence. Sadly, laws often actually help create a climate of strife and evil that perpetuates resistance to the law of love. Even when they seem necessary, laws are temporary band-aids until the ancient wound heals. Gandhi taught, "It is pure deception to believe that an evil can be eradicated by the passing of a law. What is needed is a conversion of heart."

Reflection

The next time you find yourself in a conflict, seek a "win-win" situation. Such a resolution allows both your needs and the other's to be achieved. Such reconciliation will require much more time, effort and patience than would a quick, one-sided victory.

Mindful of Jesus' words on the road to Jerusalem and Calvary, as your Lenten work today seek ways to serve the needs of others. Again, this can be a hard task. To begin, find some small, unnoticed kind act you can do for those with whom you live or work. In time you can cultivate an enjoyment for the secret service of doing hidden deeds of kindness. Enjoy, like that famous secret service agent, Santa Claus, your deeds of charity and generosity.

Prayerfully recall again the words of Isaiah that we are to *wash ourselves clean, put away our misdeeds from before God's eyes, cease doing evil and learn to do good.* For when we *make justice our aim, redress those wronged, hear the orphan's plea and defend the widow—even though our sins be like scarlet, they will become white as snow. Though they be crimson red, they will become white as wool* (see Is. 1: 2, 18).

O God, come to my assistance. O Lord, make haste to help me as I take up my Lenten allies, and my cross, to climb your holy mountain.

Second Thursday in Lent

The prophet Jeremiah gives us the chilling advice to curse the one whose heart turns away from God, like a barren bush in the desert that enjoys no change of season, but stands in a lava waste, in desolate terrain (see Jer. 17: 5-10).

Jesus tells us the parable of the rich man who ignores the beggar Lazarus at his gate (see Lk. 16: 19-31).

As you ascend in this expanding range of holy mountains, you pass through the desert of Lent with its twisted trees and bushes. The hearts of those who turn away from God are compared to barren bushes, the *krummholz*, the "crooked wood" of stunted vegetation caused by the wind at high elevations.

Let the twisted krummholz remind you that a twisted heart stands in lava waste. Each Lent you are once again called to a conversion of heart, the kind of which Gandhi spoke. That goal of healing your heart is not only the destination of the Lenten expedition but of your entire life-pilgrimage.

Such conversion of heart requires patience. Lacking confidence in the power of Jesus' Gospel message, you can be in a hurry to change society, the church or any social institution. It's easy to feel disillusioned, to feel like you're living in a barren desert, when things don't change. It can be hard to invest your heart in the slow, difficult personal task of learning to do good. Yet only when you make changing your heart your primary spiritual task will society begin to change.

That task requires becoming a martyr. It's a small death to refuse to return anger for anger or insult for insult. It's an arduous task to open your heart to allow it to be washed clean by the blood of the Lamb, Jesus' blood poured forth in love for you and for all the peoples of the world. The good news, however, is that you can do this work even here in this desert area where there is no water!

You can do your Lenten laundry in the midst of traffic when

someone's rudeness or carelessness causes impatience, the step-child of anger, to rise up in you. You can do your heart-laundry at checkout stands or at the supper table. Remember, as a wise seeker, that laundry time is temptation time. Each time you're tempted to say, "No, I'm not going to do the laundry," the evil one will whisper in your ear, "You're right! You've been offended. You must fight fire with fire. Teach them a lesson." Or in terms of today's Gospel: "You're right! You do need to hold on to your money for a rainy day—you don't want to end up like that beggar. Besides, you deserve your money!" When you hear such voices, look to your blue ribbon and pray to be delivered from evil. For each time you refuse to do the laundry, you must accept a personal responsibility for greed and exploitation, as well as for violent rape, brutal murder and the slaughter of the innocent, for you are part of spreading the disease of evil in the world.

Reflection

Read today's Gospel parable of the beggar Lazarus and the rich person who feasted splendidly every day. As in any story, it is natural to identify with one or more of the characters. With which of the two in the parable do you identify? Are you poor, neglected Lazarus or the blind, wealthy fat man?

Reflect that along with your heart, your eyes also require Lenten laundering and cleansing. Do you, like the well-fed rich person, also fail to see those at your very doorstep who are in need?

Second Friday in Lent

The book of Genesis tells us the story of Joseph, the dreamer, who is thrown into the cistern by his brothers (see Gen. 37: 3-4, 12-13, 17-28).

In the parable of the Farmer and the vineyard, Jesus tells the caretakers of the kingdom of God that it will be taken away from them and given to those who will yield a rich harvest (see Mt. 21: 33-43, 45-46).

Today for your backpack parable, you're given the story of the vineyard where the tenant farmers abused, stoned and killed the owner's servants who came to collect the owner's share of the crop. They even killed the son. And you, as a tenant farmer, a caretaker entrusted with the Gospel and the work of God—have you produced a good harvest?

Lent is memory time. Lent is a season to remember the purpose of life, to recall your primal vocation. Unlike jubilee years that come only once every twenty-five or fifty years, Lent comes each year. Like spring it is an annual awakening. As a steward of gifts, as a tenant farmer meant to work for a harvest of the seeds planted by God, you may be faced with the dilemma of crop failure or only partially filled barns. An answer for that problem of under-production lies in another backpack parable.

There was a young man hired by a state highway department. His first job was to paint white lines down the center of a highway because the automatic equipment was temporarily out of order. The highway department superintendent took him out to the place on the highway where he was to begin. Setting down the can of paint, he said to the young man, "Now, start painting the white lines here."

The first day the young man painted eight miles of the white line. The second day he painted four miles, the third day two miles, and the fourth day only one mile.

The highway superintendent was confused as to why his productivity continued to decrease daily. He called the young man into his office and asked, "Why are you painting less and less each day?" The young man responded, "I'm getting less and less done because the paint can is getting further and further away."

The further you are from the Source, the less you will accomplish in the reign of God. Daily prayer is a returning to the Sacred Source right in the midst of a society basically devoid of the sacred. At that mystic spring of prayer you are nourished and refreshed in your resolve and in your power to do good. Your dreams of helping create the kingdom of God on earth are reawakened and revitalized. With practice you can learn to carry the paint can, the mystic source with you, so that instead of decreasing, you will daily increase in doing good.

To stay close to the Source requires being creative in finding places and times of prayer and communion with God. Remember Joseph, who met God in the dry and empty cistern. Whenever you find that your Lenten works, and the work of bringing forth the reign of God, are falling off, return to the Source to be renewed.

Reflection

Today is ideal for a review of your daily practice of prayer, not only for this season of Lent but throughout the entire year. Do you pray only when you or loved ones are in need, in times of sickness or emergency?

When was the last time that you, like Jesus, escaped to a mountain-retreat, a time of withdrawal, to be regenerated?

Do you approach prayer as a duty or as a time of communion and renewal? If a return to prayer was one of your Lenten allies, how faithful have you been to that resolution?

O God, come to my assistance. O Lord, make haste to help me as I take up my Lenten allies, and my cross, to climb your holy mountain.

Second Saturday in Lent

The prophet Micah sings of the merciful Shepherd who deals compassionately with the flock that dwells apart in a woodland, in the shadow of Mount Carmel (see Mi. 7: 14-15, 18-20).

Amidst murmurs that Jesus welcomed sinners and tax collectors and ate with them, Jesus tells us the parable of the Prodigal Son (see Lk. 15: 1-3, 11-32).

Having climbed ever upward in the days of this week, you have now reached the slopes of Mount Horeb, known also as Mount Sinai, one of the holiest of holy mountains where God visited Moses in the burning bush. Tomorrow's celebration of the Third Sunday in Lent will begin with that account. In the woodland of Mount Carmel (whose name means "orchard"), which leads to tomorrow's mountain, the expedition pauses to remember just who is part of the company of our expedition.

Lent began with Jesus stating clearly that his mission and community weren't intended for the self-righteous. We see that again in this Lenten Saturday Gospel, which includes one of his most powerful and beautiful parables, the Prodigal Son. (On the fourth Sunday of Lent, you will visit this parable again, yet each time it can hold a new treasure of insights.) As a compassionate God visited the flock as a shepherd in the shadow of Mount Carmel as well as on Mount Horeb, so too Jesus visited his flock. Like a shepherd to the "prodigals" of his day, Jesus even shared meals with those in need of a healer and a friend.

As a teacher of mountain climbers, Jesus' favorite form of instruction was parables. Mindful of the climb before you, for your nourishment, here's another backpack parable:

Outside the gates of heaven, near the entrance to the Supreme-Supreme Court of Angels and Saints, there is a dressing room. It gives candidates, before the most important interview of their lives, a place to first check their appearance.

One day a good and devout woman arrived at heaven's gate. An angel directed her to the dressing room where she found four full-length mirrors. She checked her hair and makeup, and all was in order. Out of her small casket-suitcase she took her choir robe (she sang every Sunday at church). She slipped on the robe and pinned on it her good-conduct medals for piety, donations to clothing drives and Christmas charity to the poor. (During the other eleven months, however, she seldom thought of or even cared what happened to the poor, considering those on welfare to be lazy and shiftless.)

Next, she put her rosary—which she had prayed daily—in her pocket and applied to her face the rouge which glowed from the three thousand vigil candles she had lighted in her lifetime. She lifted her robe and inspected the callouses on her knees from her long hours of prayer and adoration. All was perfect. Finally, she stepped out of the door and stood before heaven's Supreme-Supreme Court.

The angels and saints hooted, booed and threw rotten eggs and tomatoes at her as they shouted, "Shame! Shame!" In tears she ran out of the courtroom. As she fled weeping, she ran past another woman at the door. The second woman was entering reluctantly since she was a sinner. She never went to church—well, almost never. She never prayed unless a crisis was at hand. She was guilty of a host of petty sins and a few large ones as well. When she entered the dressing room and opened her casket-suitcase, she discovered that it was empty!

She stood naked before the all-revealing mirrors, her face red with shame. When the angel called, "Next," she pleaded not to be sent before the court: "Please have mercy, I am a sinner. I am ashamed to appear before the saints. I am not worthy to be here."

The angel pushed her through the door anyway, and she found herself standing naked before the Supreme-Supreme Court. As one body, they all stood and applauded loud and long. A neon sign over the entrance to heaven lit up with the message, GO THIS WAY. As she approached the entrance, she saw that it was only four feet high! Above it was a sign that read *Servants Entrance. Appropriate Dress Required.*

Reflection

Take a few moments to reflect on the personal implications of this parable. If no reflections are forthcoming, consider these questions: How do you feel about having completed these first two weeks of Lent? If you're reading this, you probably feel pretty good since you're aware that most people are not even remotely involved in any practice of this season of renewal and reform—right?

How do you think you will react when you arrive in heaven and find it crowded with people known as notorious sinners? What will be your response when you see those who, like the prodigal son, repented days or even minutes before their deaths?

Will your reaction be like that of the elder brother in Jesus' parable? Or will you enjoy heaven as a great party for those who were once thought lost but who have been found, for those once thought dead but who have come back to life?

Third Sunday in Lent
Mount Horeb-Sinai

Moses comes to Mount Horeb where God appears in fire flaming from a bush. God instructs Moses to take off his shoes, for the place where he is standing is holy ground (see Ex. 3: 1-8, 13-15).

Jesus tells us the parable of a man who for three years had come to his fig tree in search of fruit without finding any. He tells his gardener to chop it down (see Lk. 13: 1-9).

Today we've reached the top of Mount Horeb-Sinai, the third peak in our ascent of the Mountain of God. Horeb-Sinai is the arch-mountain of God's shrines since it was here that God spoke out of the burning bush to Moses. Here, as well, God sealed a sacred marriage covenant with Israel amidst volcanic fire, smoke and wind.

This is another place where stunted, twisted *krummholz* trees and bushes abound. One such krummholz bush on this mountain became aflame with the Divine Mystery. Out of the fire, God spoke to Moses the sheepherder: "This is holy ground, take off your sandals." Then God sent Moses down to Egypt to be the agent of justice for the captive minorities there. Mount Horeb's divine commission to free the oppressed from their suffering would henceforth be branded upon any true and fruitful spirituality. Moses took his staff and left his sheep in order to shepherd the great escape—the exodus of God's people.

From among the straighter krummholz wood of this mountain,

select for yourself a similar walking staff. Such a walking staff would make an excellent Lenten symbol to indicate the new direction of this season. It can be a disciple's staff, a sign of your desire to reform your life in response to the way Jesus directed his disciples. A walking staff can also remind you that you are a pilgrim in life and, especially in these forty days, a pilgrim on your way to the Mountain of God.

Once travelers used staffs to fight off wild beasts and robbers. Like your blue ribbon, your staff can remind you that you have chosen to enter into combat with evil. A wooden staff, even an old broom handle, in your prayer corner can be a fruitful symbol. Having climbed for eighteen days now, the voice of evil may again whisper, "Oh, you're too busy to take time for the work of Lent. Abandon your practices; take them up next year. Next year you can really have a good Lent." Let us clutch tightly our staffs and resist that temptation; then let us heed the Lenten warning: If you think you're standing tall and upright, watch out lest you fall!

In today's Gospel parable Jesus calls us to be fruitful, not barren like the vineyard owner's fig tree. As we pause to rest on this mountaintop, ponder an old Irish parable:

One cold, damp March day, an Irish monk was having a miserable time. He came into the abbey, complaining about having to work outside in such terrible conditions. The abbot met him as he was grumbling and said to him, "You must treat uncomfortable days the same as good days." The monk only continued to grumble about having to work outside in cold weather, so the abbot said, "It's wrong to grumble, brother. You must go to confession."

When the monk went to confession, the abbot said to him, "For your penance, brother, since you grumbled about the cold and dampness, you must go to the bridge by the river. Stand under the bridge, with your staff in hand, where the water is up to your waist."

The brother didn't even get his supper. He left at once for the bridge. It was so cold standing in the water! Leaning on his staff, he remembered the abbot's closing remarks: "If you're truly sorrowful for your sins of grumbling, at dawn's first light your staff will blossom."

Leaning on his staff in the bitter cold, the monk heard the noise of something approaching on the road. Looking out from under the bridge, he saw a notorious cattle thief with a whole herd of cattle he had stolen. The thief was leading them down the road in the dark of night. As he got to the bridge, being ever watchful, the thief looked down and saw the monk standing in the icy water. The cattle thief said to the monk, "For the love of heaven, man, what are you doin' down there in the river? You should be home in your bed."

The monk responded, "Well, I grumbled about having to work outside in the rainy weather, and the abbot—ah, a hard man indeed he is—gave me this penance."

"Oh my!" the thief said. "If the abbot gave you the penance of standing all night in cold water for grumblin' about the weather, what kind of penance would he give me if I came to confession?"

The thief immediately shooed the cattle down the road and back into the pasture from which he had taken them. Then he came running down the road and jumped into the river, saying, "Move over, brother, move over!" So there the two stood, with their staffs in hand, underneath the bridge in the icy cold river. Ah, friends, if you think your Lenten penances are hard! The poor pair shivered from the cold as they nodded off to sleep leaning on their staffs.

At dawn's first light the monk awoke and immediately looked at his staff, but he saw nothing on it. He brought it toward his face as close as his eyelashes, thinking maybe the blossoms were very small. But, alas, there were no blossoms! Then he looked over at the cattle thief leaning asleep on his staff. The staff was covered with blossoms!

The story is a paradox, as twisted as any krummholz. The cattle thief, who was guilty of real sin, becomes fruitful. The sunrise found his staff blooming because he was truly sorry for his sins. The monk's staff remained as barren as his heart. While the monk had embraced his penance under obedience, he wasn't sorry for grumbling and bore a grudge in his heart against the abbot.

Reflection

This season of Lent is a call to reform and change of heart. While you can perform external penances and the other disciplines of Lent, you may not be changed by them. Ask yourself if you wish to be transformed by your Lenten exercises.

If you place a Lenten staff in your prayer corner, may its presence continuously ask you the question, "Come Easter Sunday morning at sunrise, will your Lenten staff have blossoms on it?"

Third Monday in Lent

Naaman the leper is advised by the prophet Elisha to go wash seven times in the Jordan so that his flesh might be healed and he might be clean (see 2 Kgs. 5: 1-15).

When Jesus quotes to his neighbors the proverb that no prophet is accepted in his native place, they become angry and try to throw him from the brow of the hill to his death (see Lk. 4: 24-30).

As we make our way along a ledge leading down from Mount Sinai, be cautious lest you fall to your death, just as the hometown neighbors of Jesus wished to push him off the precipice. Jesus was threatened in today's Gospel not by the priests and scribes but by his very neighbors who refused to believe in him. He angered them by challenging their poverty of faith in him and reminded them that those of other beliefs are often more open to God's ways. He pointed to Naaman, the non-Jew healed of his leprosy when he placed faith in Elisha's directions.

The Nazarenes' hearts were closed to Jesus as God's Son. Just like Jesus' neighbors, our hearts can also be tightly shut. How readily, for example, do devout Christians reject the action of God's Spirit in other religions. Yet the Vatican Council called Roman Catholics to have open and receptive hearts to all that is good and true in non-Christian religions. Christians of all churches can benefit from the words of Pope John Paul II in the document on Dialogue and Proclamation:

> While remaining firm in their belief that in Jesus Christ we have the fullness of revelation, Christians must remember that God has also been manifested to the followers of other religious traditions. Consequently, with receptive minds they must approach the convictions and values of others. Moreover, the fullness of truth received in Jesus Christ does not guarantee that they (Christians) have grasped the truth fully. While keeping their identity intact, Christians must be prepared to learn and to receive from and through others the positive values of their traditions.

A reformed heart, the goal of this Lenten Season, is always a heart open to the mysterious ways of God. Lent's call to a reform of our hearts reminds us how easily they can be closed by discrimination. While having embraced Jesus Christ as our savior, we must seek the universality of God's truth. As our expedition descends from Sinai, the holy mountain of Judaism, let us pray for hearts that are receptive to all the ways of God. Let us be open to learn from the spiritual traditions, prayers and practices of Jews, Moslems, Hindus and Buddhists as seekers of the fullness of the Truth.

Reflection

Take a few moments and pause to examine your religious discriminations. Do you grant respect and openness toward other religious pathways even if they are not your personal way to God?

If you believe that God is only revealed in Jesus Christ and are not open to learning about God from non-Christian religions, is your heart like those of the Nazarenes?

O God, come to my assistance. O Lord, make haste to help me as I take up my Lenten allies, and my cross, to climb your holy mountain.

Third Tuesday in Lent

Azariah prays that, with a contrite heart and humble spirit, God's people will be received by God (see Dn. 3: 25, 34-43).

Jesus calls his disciples to have a heart willing to forgive not seven times, but seventy times seven times. He tells the parable of the royal official whose debts were graciously pardoned, but who refused to pardon the minor debts of a lower official (see Mt. 18: 21-35).

Lent is a time of rebirth, another name for reform. Horace, the Roman poet who lived shortly before Christ, said, "The mountains will be in labor, and a ridiculous mouse will be brought forth." What a waste this Lenten season of rebirth will be if only a "church mouse" is brought forth and there is no true reformation. Church mice are the pious who leave their religion behind when they venture forth from their churchly environment.

Climbers know that getting one's heart together with one's feet is often a challenge. Many find it easy to walk to church but leave their hearts at home or at the office. It's easier to quickly pronounce a blessing on your enemies who speak evil about you than to really refrain from bearing a grudge against them.

True forgiveness involves the whole person: body and mind, memory and heart. A humble spirit is one eager to forgive—and one that first looks in the mirror before passing judgment on another. At the Redstone Arsenal in Huntsville, Alabama, the U.S. Army guided missile school, an inspection was being conducted by a particularly tough colonel. The colonel stopped at one soldier, and after looking him up and down he said with a scowl, "Trooper, button that pocket!" The soldier stammered, "Right now, sir?" The colonel snapped back, "Of course, right now!" Whereupon the soldier very carefully reached out and buttoned the flap on the colonel's shirt pocket.

Recall Jesus' words about noticing the splinter in another's eye while remaining blind to a two-by-four plank in one's own eye. We need to face the fact that we are hypocrites if we fail to remove the planks from our own eyes first (see Mt. 7: 1-5). The royal steward in today's parable was pardoned his great debt, yet he refused to see that he should grant pardon for the debt that was owed him. One of the most difficult Lenten penances is to refuse to judge others and to constantly pardon those who offend you.

The human mind seems addicted to making judgments and resists forgiving. Nations, groups and individuals nurse to their breasts old wounds, injuries and grievances. A contrite heart is humbled by an awareness of the guilt of its own failings. The origin of our English word *contrite* is the Latin term for "being bruised." Hard hearts resist bruising, even when they've been broken. Hard hearts likewise reject showing compassion and pardon toward others. Blessed are those with black-and-blue bruised hearts, for they shall be compassionate.

Reflection

Is your heart black-and-blue, bruised by an awareness of your sins and failings? If it is bruiseless, consider letting your heart become a punching bag for former sins. Recall your former mistakes and failures at fidelity and allow these memories to soften up your heart. Being bruised, your heart will be eager to forgive again and again and again.

Third Wednesday in Lent

Moses tells the people, and us, to hear God's statutes and live by them so that we can truly live. He advises us to take care and not let them slip out of our memory (see Dt. 4: 1, 5-9).

Jesus says that he has not come to destroy religion or the Law, but to fulfill them. To be great in heaven, we should teach the commandments by living them (see Mt. 5: 17-19).

Recall last Sunday's parable of the barren fig tree. That teaching-story was directed at those most zealous for the law of God: the Pharisees, scribes and priests. The story is a "naughty" teaching of Jesus implying that they weren't productive, that they were just living off the land and its people. Instead of saying, "Let's water the tree and put fresh soil around it," the gardener says, "Let's put manure around it." Scripture scholar Dr. John Pilch says that undoubtedly the crowd roared with laughter at the idea of their clergy being surrounded with manure to make them fruitful. Jesus didn't propose sanitized chemical fertilizer, but good, old-fashioned animal manure. Consider standing in that for 365 days! Then Jesus adds, like a real revolutionary, "And if, after that, they don't become fruitful, chop 'em down! Off with their heads!"

Perhaps you are familiar with that African-American saying, "There can be no fire in the pew if there's ice in the pulpit." Fruitfulness and fire are cousin images. If there's no fire in the teacher's lectern, there will be no fire in the desks of students. If there's no fire in the hearts of parents, there can be no fire in family prayer or in their children's faith.

While it's easy to smile and enjoy Jesus' fig-tree anticlerical joke, it's also necessary to examine your own fig tree. Is it aflame with the love of God as was Moses' burning bush? Is it fruitful or barren?

Reflection

In the Near East fig trees bear fruit ten months out of the year. You can go to them almost any time and find fruit on them. How fruitful is your life? How creative is your marriage, your profession or work? When you pray, does your prayer consume you like fire consumed the burning bush?

Fruitfulness and creativity require time, effort and love. Are you willing to invest your work, marriage, friendships and other commitments with this trinity of fruitfulness?

O God, come to my assistance. O Lord, make haste to help me as I take up my Lenten allies, and my cross, to climb your holy mountain.

Third Thursday in Lent

Jeremiah speaks of God's call that we walk in all the ways that God has commanded so that we may prosper and be fruitful (see Jer. 7: 23-28).

Jesus casts out of a man a devil which made him mute. Jesus' enemies thereupon charge him with being an agent of the devil. Jesus says that a kingdom divided against itself is laid waste and that those who are not with him are against him (see Lk. 11: 14-23).

Since we began our ascent, we have been *freeclimbing*, a mountaineering term for climbing without the aid of pitons, ropes or other technical assistance. Today, for safety, we are roped together as we travel along an *escarpment*, a sheer cliff. Look at your blue ribbon, since demons and particularly Beelzebub, the prince of devils, lurks along this escarpment. Among the evil spirits we each must daily face and then drive out or exorcise is the fierce demon of anger. This devil easily grips our tongue and prevents us from speaking with the love and pardon of Christ.

In the presence of injustice, we rightly find justification for an angry fire blazing in our hearts; and are there not a variety of social evils to be zealous about? Yet that fire must be handled with great care, for it isn't easy to convert the energy of the fiery demon of anger. Both Jesus and Buddha warned against anger in the heart since it so easily sours the soul and disfigures us.

Once there lived a religious woman who was strongly anti-abortion, antipornography, and opposed to all imaginable social evils. She was also angry that as a woman she wasn't allowed full participation in the ministry of the Church. A good Christian woman, she prayed daily. One day in prayer, she had a private revelation that Jesus Christ was going to appear to her on Thursday at 3 P.M. Excited and overwhelmed with joy, she cleaned her entire house and had her hair done. Wearing her best dress, she waited patiently. At three o'clock the doorbell rang. She opened the front door to find an angry, bitter, scowling man. Surprised, she asked, "Who are you?" The man said, "It's three o'clock; weren't you expecting me?" Taken aback, she said, "You can't be the real Jesus Christ!" He responded, "You're absolutely right. I'm not the real Christ, but I am the Christ that others see in you!"

Reflection

Who do others see when they see you? Do they see the compassion of Christ? Do they see the smiling face of the gentle prophet Jesus who showed anger only toward the pious hypocrites and the self-righteous?

Has that tongue-tying demon of anger recently made you mute in sulking silence after you've been offended by another's words or actions? When this happens again, consider creating your own private exorcism to release your tongue. Conversely, have you exercised power to quickly gain the upper hand over someone— as a way of not having to face your own demon of anger? Likewise, consider casting that demon out.

Third Friday in Lent

The prophet Hosea says that the splendor of God shall be like the fruitful olive tree, that God's presence will smell like the Lebanon cedar (see Hos. 14: 2-10).

Jesus tells us that we are not far from God's reign when we love God with all our heart, soul, mind and strength, and our neighbor as ourself (see Lk. 11: 14-23).

This Lenten Friday, as we descend, we set up *bivouac*, a makeshift shelter, near an orchard on the side of Mount Horeb. This grove is filled with olive, fig and cedar trees. In the center of the orchard is a tall and most special tree named *love*. It is the great cedar tree of God's orchard, and outward from it grow the limbs of all the commandments of God. If a religious law springs from anywhere else but love, we can question if it is truly God's law.

St. Bernard of Clairvaux, the saintly poet of mystic love, wrote, "Love is self-sufficient: it is pleasing to itself and on its own account." When faced with the first and greatest commandment of love, we can ask the classic American question, "What's in it for me?" St. Bernard has answered our question: "Love is its own payment; love is its own reward."

The saintly Charles de Foucauld wrote in a letter what he felt was most important for good prayer: "What must come first in all prayers, however varied they may be, and what gives them real value is the love with which they are made."

Prayer is among the greatest allies of our Lenten ascent, and many of us are dissatisfied with the way we pray. There is a restlessness that leads us to find a new and better method of prayer. And there is no shortage of "new" prayer styles and techniques: Zen meditation, Centering, Charismatic prayer.... The desire to pray better is important in the work of reforming our hearts. Yet it's easy to miss the mark in the lifelong search for the perfect way to pray.

If our prayers are made out of love, they will be good prayers even if they seem otherwise to us. If we begin them with love, fill them with love and end them with love, they will be fruitful prayers. Bernard and de Foucauld are reliable mountain guides. They agree that the only reward of prayer is prayer, even when what we seek is not given, even when we find no peace in the stillness of our prayer.

Reflection

If your walking staff is to bloom, it—along with your prayers, Lenten works and devotions—must be filled with love. Take a few moments to see if these allies are indeed love-filled in your life.

Consciously begin each prayer not on your lips but in your heart and fill it with as much love as you can. Make each *amen* a love-soaked conclusion to your prayer.

O God, come to my assistance. O Lord, make haste to help me as I take up my Lenten allies, and my cross, to climb your holy mountain.

Third Saturday in Lent

God tells us that it is love that's desired, not sacrifice or holocausts. The prophet Hosea calls us to return to God, for God will heal us (see Hos. 6: 1-6).

Jesus addresses the self-righteous, who hold others in contempt, with a parable: A Pharisee and a tax collector were in prayer. The Pharisee piously thanked God that he was not like the tax collector or other sinners. Justified in his own eyes, the Pharisee was not justified in the eyes of God (see Lk. 18: 9-14).

The long journey of this week is about to end. Tomorrow we will come to our second major encampment, located at Gilgal on Jericho's plain. As a pilgrim in this new Lent, you might well be proud at how you are investing these days with a new spirit of reform instead of penance. The past thirty years have seen numerous reforms in worship and liturgy; today's parable of the haughty Pharisee and the humble toll collector can inspire another needed liturgical change. At the beginning of the Eucharistic Liturgy, the Penance Rite could be replaced by this new *Glory to God* hymn:

> Glory to God in the highest,
> > but, gee, ain't I good and pious.
> I meditate and pray at least every day,
> > and four-letter words I never ever say.
>
> Glory to God in the highest,
> > but, gee, ain't I good and pious.
> I never killed anyone when I was young,
> > though I have slaughtered quite a few with my tongue.
>
> Glory to God in the highest,
> > but, gee, ain't I good and pious.
> I never had an abortion, thank God,
> > but sex for me is *ugh*—dirty and odd.

Each day of the ascent is a challenge. Today's task is to never compare ourselves with others or consider ourselves better than others, regardless of their social standing. Never judge another's path, saying, "Look at that one's spirituality; it's as crooked as a krummholz—like it's been twisted by the mountain winds!"

Instead of looking at another's path, look at your own prayer life. Is it crooked because it lacks balance? Does your concern for morality, especially sexual morality, match your concern for justice and peace? Are your personal efforts at justice and peace pursued with the same zeal as your prayer and worship?

Look with eyes of reality upon the world. In any cause or group, there are people with good hearts and people with bad hearts. Even among oppressors and nonreligious, there are people with good hearts. While we may be eager for reformation, let us remember one of the most dangerous facts about reformations and revolutions: The oppressed almost always take on the ways of the oppressors. Righteous reformers usually become worse than their predecessors.

We've climbed now for more than three full weeks. The temptation will be to look back and down at those who haven't moved an inch since Ash Wednesday. The temptation will be to feel good about ourselves. Resist that temptation lest you lose your footing and fall. Instead, turn to God with a humble heart so that you may be truly whole.

Reflection

On this last day of the week, recall prayerfully the lessons of these Lenten days. Remember the story of the monk and the cattle thief under the bridge and pray for a reformed heart. Pray that on Easter your Lenten climbing staff will bloom.

Reflect again on the story of the woman who met an angry, spiteful Christ at her door. Ask yourself what kind of Christ others see in you.

In approaching the second half of Lent, strive to invest your service, prayer and Lenten exercises with as much love as possible. Be confident as you do that your love will make them fruitful.

Fourth Sunday in Lent
Gilgal Valley

The prophet Joshua tells us that the Israelites encamped at Gilgal on the plains of Jericho, where they celebrated the Passover (see Jos. 5: 9. 10-12).

St. Paul announces that God has given us the ministry of reconciliation, making us ambassadors of Christ (see 2 Cor. 5: 17-21).

The scribes and Pharisees murmur that Jesus welcomes sinners and eats with them, so Jesus tells them the parable of the Prodigal Son (see Lk. 15: 1-3, 11-32).

This Sunday finds our expedition at the halfway point. This is the twenty-sixth day of continuous climbing since we left base camp on Ash Wednesday. In the old, harsh penitential Lent, this Sunday was a midpoint opportunity to rejoice and to relax from one's difficult penances. We will set up camp two, located on your map at Gilgal, on the plains of Jericho across the Jordan River. Here we will lay down our backpacks and pilgrim staffs to rest and also to resupply for the path ahead. Today's rest is necessary—we will need our strength, for from now on the terrain will be more difficult.

As climbers we face, today, the paradoxical cardinal rule of mystical ascent: The only way up is down! That principle of upside-down ascent is also found in the Apostles Creed: "He suffered under Pontius Pilate, was crucified, died and was buried. *He descended into hell*, and on the third day he arose again." The

70

explanation over the centuries for this descent has been that after his death and before his resurrection, Jesus went down to a limbo-like place to bring back to God all those who had died in faith before Jesus came. These underworld detainees were the holy ones of the First Testament, saints such as Rebecca and Moses, Jeremiah and Ruth.

For us personally, that statement of faith from the Creed now indicates the new direction of our ascent of the Mountain of God when we leave camp two. That direction is simple: the Pascal journey involves going to hell. While everyone is eager to go to heaven, few are eager to go to hell on their way to heaven! As we prepare to descend into hell so as to ascend to paradise, it's important to hang on to your blue ribbon. It has been your reminder of the presence of evil and a symbol of protection from the evil one. Hell is the address of the devil and also the place where sinners suffer for their sins. Hold on to your blue ribbon because this Sunday's Gospel-parable of the Prodigal Son includes a journey to hell.

Jesus tells the parable to explain why he violated the Law and associated—even ate—with those judged to be alienated from God by their sinful lives. Particularly in Jesus' culture, anyone alienated from religious worship and social acceptance indeed lived in a hell on earth. According to the scribes and religious leaders, Jesus too sinned by his choice of table companions. No pious, law-observing Jew would ever associate—and certainly would not share the family table—with those who were not keeping the Law.

We good Christians usually don't associate with sinners either, lest by our friendship we might appear to approve of their sinful behavior. It's not that long ago when if a daughter or son married someone who had been divorced, the parents weren't allowed to attend the ceremony or even to give a gift. Such expressions of love were forbidden because they were seen as a sanction of the wayward child's sin.

Today, some might say that Jesus' reason for eating with sinners was to convert them. I don't know about you, but I've been around righteous reformers, and I do not enjoy their company!

Sharing dinner with a reformer whose main dish is my conversion is not my idea of a pleasant meal! The Gospels, however, show that those judged as sinners loved to associate with Jesus. Would they have been so eager to eat with him if he had preached to them or condemned their behavior? Sinners loved his company simply because he loved them! They knew he accepted them the way they were with an unconditional love, which, paradoxically, is the most reforming of all attitudes.

Reflection

Rest on this day, for tomorrow you will take up your difficult upside-down ascent. At this second encampment, all climbers are given a choice to either continue their ascent or to go back. Will you decide to abandon the ascent because it's too difficult to go on?

If you choose to continue, check again your allies chosen at the base camp. Have they proved to be true allies—real supports for your reform? Have you been faithful in your discipline of practising them?

If you've found that they haven't been as helpful as you thought, why not discard them? Take up new and more useful allies for the second half of the ascent. Then examine well your ally-equipment. In the difficult days ahead, take with you only what will be of service.

Fourth Monday in Lent

Isaiah tells us of God's vision of creating new heavens and a new earth, where things of the past will not be remembered (see Is. 65: 17-21).

A royal official asks Jesus to cure his child. When Jesus tells him that his son will live, with great faith the official returns to his home (see Jn. 4: 43-54).

We see in today's Gospel story how well Jesus was able to create heaven on earth. It supplements this week's visionary parable of the Prodigal Son in providing the ingredients of Jesus' recipe for turning hell into paradise: complete faith, complete forgiveness and complete love.

The father in the Prodigal Son story killed a fatted calf or young cow, which scholars say would have fed a hundred people. The father, it appeared, planned to invite the entire village to the party welcoming home his son, including all his neighbors with their wagging tongues. Surely they'd been talking about him, gossiping about the worthless son who had shamed his father. Lacking any kind of social security, the children in Jesus' society traditionally cared for their aged parents from their inheritance. This bad apple, however, this black-sheep son, had wasted his entire inheritance—and, therefore, his parent's social security!

Neighbors—then, as today—find secret pleasure in keeping track of the misfortunes and shame of others. When it comes to others' mistakes, we invariably have long memories! The story of Fred Snodgrass is a perfect example. Fred Snodgrass was a famous baseball player for the New York Giants and was on their 1912 World Series team. In the deciding game he missed a pop fly; his error allowed the winning run to come home, costing the Giants the Series. In 1974 Fred Snodgrass died. The *New York Times* headline read: **Fred Snodgrass, 85, Dead. Baseball Player Muffed Fly in 1912.** At the end of his life, what was remembered about him was his error that cost his team the World Series. After leaving baseball, he had become mayor of a city in California, was a successful rancher and banker, and a father with a wonderful family. Yet, sadly, what was remembered was his mistake!

We do the same each time we define others by their real or supposed mistakes: "She's a hard worker, but she's had two divorces. She's an ex-nun...belongs to AA...had a nervous breakdown. He's committed adultery. He's an ex-priest...went bankrupt...died of AIDS." Society too often frames people's images with their mistakes and sins. Yet the father of the prodigal son is *good news*; he's an image of God because he has holy amnesia! He doesn't remember the past sins of his son and runs to embrace him. "Give him the best robe," the father shouts with joy. "Put a ring on his finger and shoes on his feet." (Only sons wore shoes; servants went barefoot.) Then the father kissed the son, the ultimate sign of a love fueled by total absolution, without any penance or probation period.

The Gospels tell that Jesus taught by means of parables. Why has the teaching at the heart of this parable taken so long to be understood and accepted? Why are we still doing penance for our sins in Lent? The father asked his son to perform no penance other than to embrace his unconditional pardon and love. Jesus' parable crafts the greatest of all good news: God's unconditional love of us if we only come home.

If we enjoy the company of those who live outside the law, we will need to develop the skill of *traversing*, a mountain-climber's term for moving sideways across the face of a cliff. Since our society judges us by the company we keep, it's necessary to traverse with an awareness of the dangers that Jesus faced daily on his ascent.

Reflection

Are you able to imitate the father in the parable and grant unconditional pardon to those who may have shamed and offended you, to those who have broken your trust?

Are you willing to traverse the dangerous path of befriending those who are outcasts in society and the church?

O God, come to my assistance. O Lord, make haste to help me as I take up my Lenten allies, and my cross, to climb your holy mountain.

Fourth Tuesday in Lent

The prophet Ezekiel describes a vision of water flowing from underneath the threshold of the temple toward the east. Soon it is a river which can be crossed only by swimming (see Ez. 47: 1-9, 12).

A sick man who had waited thirty-eight years at the Pool of Bethesda to be cured of his sickness tells Jesus that he wants to be healed but has no one to plunge him into the pool once the water has been stirred up. On that Sabbath day, Jesus tells the invalid to stand up, pick up his mat and walk (see Jn. 5: 1-3, 5-16).

A river flows through this desert valley of our second camp. The river should be the Jordan, but it isn't. It's the dark, foul-smelling River Styx. In classical mythology this is the river that flows nine times around the infernal regions. At the shore waits the ferry of the hideous boatman Charon, who escorts the spirits of the dead across the Styx into hell.

In the coming days, our journey will follow the banks of the Styx as it enters a great underground cavern. The upside-down rule of our ascent requires that we must now descend into the underworld, following the tracks of Jesus who came this way before us. Like him, we also must enter hell if we are to reach the top of Mount Easter.

Ron Rollheiser, a Canadian priest and author, writes beautifully of a new image of Jesus' descent into hell. If, as he says, hell is alienation from God, then Jesus entered into that hellish alienation on his cross. From that tree of hell he cried, "My God, my God, where are you? Why have you abandoned me?" No voice came from a cloud, saying, "You are my beloved son, and I'm really proud of what you're doing." It wasn't only on the cross, however, that Jesus descended into hell. He did so each time he entered into the private hells of those who had been alienated as outcasts of society and religion.

Only one who knew firsthand the pain of alienation could create such a beautiful parable as the Prodigal Son. Jesus knew the pain of alienation from family, village, religion and even God! The cross of Christ loses its power if Jesus was in the embrace of God as he hung on it! The absence of God (for all practical purposes) from Mount Calvary truly makes the cross a hanging hell.

Following the underground river deeper into the bowels of

the mountains, we come to the place of ordination for those who aspire to be ministers of reconciliation: hell. The vocation to be ambassadors of God and of Christ's love requires entering the private and public hells of others. Hell, then, is appropriate as the ordination site of such a minister of God.

Our dangerous descent deeper into this netherworld is like a *glissade*, the process in which hikers slide down a slope on the soles of their feet. Sliding into hell as ambassadors of God's love requires excellent balance and agility as well as a love that's devoid of vengeance and judgment.

Reflection

This Lenten Tuesday's reflection is a glissade parable, a true story of a couple who lived in West Virginia. They were good Christians who raised chickens. Unfortunately, their chickens were always going over into the neighbors' yard and scratching in the flower beds, which angered the neighbors. Even after the couple had built a fence, the chickens continued to find a way into the neighbors' yard.

One Sunday upon returning from church, the couple found all of their chickens dead. Their necks had been rung, apparently because one too many times they had gotten into the flower beds. Later that afternoon there was a knock at the neighbors' door. Opening their door, they found the couple standing there with a big platter of fried chicken. The woman said, "We had more chicken than we could eat today, and we thought you might enjoy some."

Fourth Wednesday in Lent

Isaiah speaks of God's pledge to never forget us. God promises to cut a road through all the holy mountains and to make the highways level (see Is. 49: 8-15).

Jesus says that an hour is coming when all those in tombs shall come forth when they hear his voice (see Jn. 5: 17-30).

At midweek, we prepare to leave the hellish River Styx. Before us is a *chimney*, a narrow vertical passageway in the rock wall. Climbing this cramped passageway is like being in a vertical tomb—and what is more tomb-like than the hellish space of those who feel alienated from God? Into those burial places of the living dead we are called to go as God's ambassadors so that they can hear the voice of Christ calling them forth. Hell can be as close as next door or even the next room; it's the residence of anyone with whom we are at odds, who is angry at us, envious or competitive with us or lost in painful judgments.

We are ambassadors of the peace of heaven each time we face, with unconditional love, any of these attitudes in others. We go to them not as accusers but as ambassadors of reconciliation. To approach those whom we know may harbor hate for us means walking into the hell of their anger and negativity. However, it is in these hellish places that we are ordained as ministers of reconciliation. In the fiery anger of others, we can feel God's hand upon our heads, ordaining us to this ministry of martyrdom. The ceremony of ordination begins when Jesus presents us with our passports, saying, "Come, follow me, and go to hell."

Frequently, ambassadors are called upon to do things for their country that they normally would not choose. For example, President Teddy Roosevelt invited the French Ambassador Jules Jusserand to accompany him on one of his "point-to-point" walks. These walks were legendary in Washington since the president insisted that no obstacle be circumvented; one was to go through or over anything that blocked the way. On their walk, Teddy Roosevelt and Ambassador Jusserand came to the Potomac River. They stripped and were about to plunge into the water when the president noticed that the ambassador was still wearing his white gloves. Roosevelt turned and said, "Mr. Ambassador, have you forgotten to remove your gloves?" "Oh no, Monsieur President! What if we should meet some ladies?"

Reflection

Do you think that you have a vocation to the ministry of reconciliation, to be a witness to God's unconditional and non-judgmental love? As an ambassador, do you have certain limits with regard to being stripped for love, even if those limits are only your white gloves?

If you aspire to be a minister of God's reconciliation, realize that it may require being stripped of the white gloves of polite society. It may also mean facing and reconciling in yourself the same difficult and painful states of anger, envy and judgment that you are striving to forgive in others.

O God, come to my assistance. O Lord, make haste to help me as I take up my Lenten allies, and my cross, to climb your holy mountain.

Fourth Thursday in Lent

Because they had made a golden calf, worshiping and sacrificing to it, God cries out at how stiff-necked are the people who had been rescued and brought out of Egypt (see Ex. 32: 7-14).

Asked by the religious leaders to explain himself, Jesus says that the very works which he performs are his witnesses and give testimony on his behalf that it is God who has sent him (see Jn. 5: 31-47).

Each time Jesus went into the hell of an outcast or sinner, he did so because God had sent him there. God sends, or rather invites, us to go to hell as well. Many refuse, being too busy, too busy worshiping the golden calves of their good and honorable names. As the Israelites constructed an idol of a golden calf, we can as easily make an idol of our glowing, golden public image and proceed to worship it.

As God sent Jesus to those who were alienated and separated

from God, so we too are sent. "Come, follow me and be one with all who feel alienated from God," says the Friend of sinners. Images of Jesus as a friend and companion of sinners may not seem shocking—as long as the sinners are found only in biblical times! It's more of a test to make contemporary his descents into hell.

Picture a modern abortion clinic outside of which is a crowd of angry demonstrators shouting condemnations. Out of the clinic comes a fifteen-year-old black girl who's just had an abortion. Walking beside her through the gauntlet of angry shouts is Jesus. Image the scene of a gay bar at which sits Jesus, drinking and laughing with those present. Shape in your mind an image of a whorehouse in Tijuana, Mexico, in which Jesus sits visiting with the women who work there. Picture the home of a couple living together but not married; enjoying a meal with them at their table is Jesus. You might even imagine Jesus in the company of rapists, robbers and others who seriously victimize and exploit.

The ministry of reconciliation is as much *good news* today as it was when that ministry was first practiced by Jesus. Brave and loyal disciples are those who can say, "I will go to hell for those I love, and for a stranger as well. With the grace of God, I can love and support them without having to condemn or affirm their behavior." Whenever we go to hell to be living messengers of God's unconditional love, we can trust we are following in the footsteps of Jesus the Reconciler.

Reflection

Do you own a golden calf? Do you worship a polished, proper social image-idol which prevents you from becoming a minister of reconciliation to a son or daughter, friend or neighbor?

Which of these is for you a more powerful drive: (1) To point out to others their mistakes or sins? (2) To love others without judgment or reprimand?

When was the last time you felt you had gone into hell for someone?

Fourth Friday in Lent

The wicked speak of their desire to condemn the "self-styled child of God" to a shameful death to see if God will come to the rescue (see Wis. 2: 1, 12-22).

Jesus decides not to travel in Judea because some there were looking for a chance to kill him (see Jn. 7: 1-2, 10. 25-30).

After several days of our underground journey, we emerge through the *chimney* tunnel. As we do, we affirm the truth of the upside-down rule that the best way to ascend is to descend. Today we find ourselves halfway up the side of the Mount of Olives.

Ringing in the fresh air are Isaiah's words about *how beautiful upon the mountains are the feet of those who sing the good news of peace* (see Is. 52: 7), the peace of reconciliation with God. May each of us on this expedition find that our feet are beautiful because they are willing to carry the message of peace even into hell.

Looking up, we see that dark storm clouds of hate are swirling around the Mount of Olives, and around the gentle reconciler, Jesus. Two weeks from today, his enemies won't need to look any further for a chance to kill him. On Good Friday, on another mount, he will die a shameful death. On that day, God will not step in to rescue him from his painful personal hell. More painful than the nails will be the stripping away of his honor and dignity. More piercing than the thorns will be the shame of dying a disgraceful death.

If we wish to be ministers of God's peace, we need to know in advance that it can mean the loss of our dignity. In the parable that has been our source of nourishment this week, before the lost son can reach home, the father runs down the road to meet him. In the Near East elders never run. By running, the old father shows a lack of concern for dignity. Jesus suggests that God will run to meet halfway any black sheep who wants to return home.

How many prodigals have started for home, only to be met by family and friends with scorn and a shaking finger of shame? How many prodigals have headed for home and for God, only to be met with icy rejection unless they beg for pardon, shame themselves and embrace a heavy penance?

In the act of being nailed to his cross, Jesus offers to each of his disciples the priestly ministry of reconciliation. Do not turn away from such a heroic ministry because of a fear of social disgrace. As we ascend the Mount of Olives, look for a *belay*, a rock to which climbers can cling or tie themselves for security. Your belay is the rock of the cross, a sign of the defeat and ultimate victory of Christ. Place your faith in that belay and, without hesitation, descend into the hells and alienations of others.

As a verb, *belay* refers to holding or securing a rope for a companion climber. Each time we descend into another's hell, we offer to belay, to pull the person out. We can do so without fear because Christ is our belay, and Christ himself has lowered us into hell. Fear not, we will be safely and victoriously pulled up and out of hell.

Reflection

One more day remains in this extremely difficult fourth week of Lent. Can you feel the presence of Christ, the divine belay, as you contemplate entering into the hell of others' alienation from society, the church or God?

Can you also enter as reconciler into the hells of suffering felt by the jobless, homeless and hungry, the outcasts of society?

Take off your shoes and look at your feet. Are they beautiful? Do your feet carry good or bad news?

O God, come to my assistance. O Lord, make haste to help me as I take up my Lenten allies, and my cross, to climb your holy mountain.

Fourth Saturday in Lent

Like a trusting lamb being led to the slaughter, Jeremiah had not realized that his enemies were hatching death plots against him (see Jer. 11: 18-20).

The crowds are all sharply divided over Jesus, saying that the Messiah is not going to come from Galilee. However, not a person dares to lay hands on him (see Jn. 7: 40-53).

The cartoon character Pogo once said, "We are confronted by insurmountable opportunities!" How true is that wisdom for us as we climb today and each day of our lives. Looking back on our descent and journey through hell shows us how hard it is to be a minister of reconciliation. When faced with the insurmountable, may we have climber's vision to see life's obstacles as great opportunities.

This Saturday we need to begin using the technique of *switchbacking*, zigzagging to counter the steep slopes we are climbing. To switchback instead of climbing straight up the slope of the Mount of Olives may appear to be extra work, going the long way. However, it's the most efficient way to climb when confronted with the insurmountable. Zigzagging from the company of saints to the company of sinners is the way to be in full communion with Christ.

If our contemporary community of disciples of the Risen Jesus excludes those living outside the law, sinners and those on the margins of society, is it truly a Community of Christ? If we are only willing to associate with the good, pious and morally "correct," can we claim membership in the full Body of Christ?

Storm clouds swirl around Mount Moriah and Mount Zion with its great temple. Tomorrow, Jesus will go to the temple to enter into the hell of a poor woman caught in the act of adultery. In the gathering storm clouds, his enemies are plotting to trap him as one who is against God's Law, one bent on destroying their religion.

Reflection

In the *Hail Mary* we ask the Mother of God, "Pray for us sinners now and at the hour of our death." Does that penitential petition apply to you or just to others?

As a Lenten prayer today, repeat that one line from the *Hail Mary* over and over to yourself as you walk trustingly with Christ toward his hour of death.

Fifth Sunday in Lent
The Mount of Olives

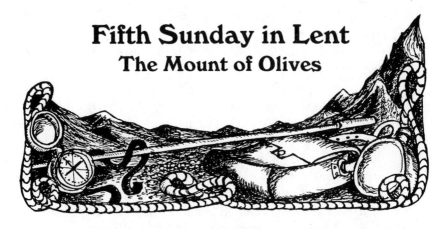

God speaks of making a way in the desert where wild beasts will honor God, even the jackals and ostriches (see Is. 43: 16-21).

Paul says that he gives no thought to what lies behind, rather he pushes on ahead (see Phil. 3: 8-14).

Jesus asks the woman if anyone has condemned her. Neither, then, does he condemn her. He tells her to depart in peace and sin no more (see Jn. 8: 1-11).

This is the thirty-third day of the ascent; seven days more will bring us to the high ridge of Holy Week. As we ascend the Mount of Olives, we face a fear of all climbers: an avalanche of rocks and stones. Like Paul, let us give no thought to what lies behind us, and even with the fear of an avalanche, let us push onward as our expedition ascends this holy mount.

Also facing us between here and the summit of Mount Easter are a variety of wild beasts. As Jesus met them in his desert Lent, so will we. Yet that fearful encounter gives us an opportunity to add two more symbols to our celebration of the new Lent. Along with our blue ribbon and pilgrim staff we now have two Lenten mascots. They are the wild beasts Isaiah says will honor God: the desert jackal and the ostrich. While on the surface not nearly as attractive, we will explore how they may be the Lenten equivalent of the Easter rabbit.

Cousins to our coyotes, jackals travel in packs and also howl at night. Both ostriches and jackals, because of their high-pitched, howling calls, have been used in describing mourners: "They wail like jackals and ostriches." Jackals inhabit the wastelands and old ruins. They are scavengers, living off dead animals and eating the garbage of villages.

In today's Gospel, Jesus descends from the Mount of Olives and goes up to the temple on Mount Moriah. There, a pack of jackals—the pious Pharisees and scribes—drag before him a woman they caught in the act of adultery. They shame her in front of everyone as she awaits the deadly avalanche of stones to be thrown at her. Cast into a living hell of shame, she is joined by Jesus. Presently, both are encircled by the jackals.

The poor woman is caught in a trap where the issue isn't so much sexual misconduct as property and honor. Women are central in cases of adultery in some Mediterranean societies only because they are considered to be the property of their husbands. Having sex with another's wife is an act of robbing and shaming her husband.

In the Near East, jackals are called "street cleaners" because they eat the refuse from the streets. In John's Gospel the scribes, like those animal street cleaners, come dragging what they considered to be trash into the temple area. Yet something doesn't smell right about the scene. The woman has been caught in the midst of adultery, an act which requires two persons. So where is the guilty man? The law in Deuteronomy requires that both the man and woman be stoned to death. The law also states that for a charge of adultery two witnesses plus the husband must be present. Since it would have been difficult for the guilty man to escape from the husband and at least two witnesses, this scene reeks of the garbage of foul play.

Reflection

As you continue your ascent into the fifth week of Lent, let today's Gospel be a warning. Beware, if you are tempted to be a zealot! Beware, if you want to throw stones and condemn others. Make sure that you know the whole story and that your motives—and your heart—are clean.

Do you hold a stone in your hand, eager to condemn another? Do you enjoy being part of an avalanche, adding your stones of gossip to be rained down on some poor victim? Regardless of the gravity of another's sin, are you free enough of sin to participate in the stoning?

Fifth Monday in Lent

Condemned to death, Susanna prays to God. Her prayer is answered when a young boy named Daniel cries out that he will have no part in the woman's death (see Dn. 13: 41-62).

Jesus asks the woman where everyone has gone. Since no one is left to condemn her, then neither does Jesus (see Jn. 8: 1-11).

Today's Gospel repeats yesterday's and requires that we face that Scripture passage squarely with a mountain-climber's courage. On a mountain it requires no effort to find a stone to throw, the ground is covered with them. Furthermore, the life-journey in contemporary culture has a high avalanche risk since we live in one of the most stone-throwing of times. From the left and the right, all kinds of stones come raining down in angry verbal attacks, condemnations and violent demonstrations of a new vindictive puritanism.

Few are spared from being struck with stones thrown by feminists, antifeminists, antiabortionists, radical environmentalists, antihomosexuals, anti-African Americans, anti-Jews, anti-Asians. Often the theologically orthodox and fundamentalists pelt with stones those who seek change and reform. And reformers throw stones back. None are safe; even parents come under a hail of stones as adult-children accuse them of failures to nurture or love them properly.

Before casting a stone, we are well advised to consider Jesus' first law of stone-throwing: "If you are free of sin, you can throw the first stone." Akin to it is the first law for sanctimonious street cleaners: "Before you go out and clean up society of immorality or indecency, first clean up your heart and your home." Challenged by such self-examination, we can be like the other wild beast of this fifth Lenten week and bury our heads in the sand. That ostriches bury their heads in the sand is actually a myth. However, there is no myth in how easily we are blinded to our own faults and failings.

Desert ostriches are called "camel birds" because they are seven to eight feet tall, weighing as much as three hundred pounds, yet they are able to run up to fifty miles per hour. The ostrich, however, seems to lack common sense—when it is attacked, it runs in circles, making capture easy. We too tend to run around in circles when we are attacked or when we're obsessed about pet causes, like abortion, ecology or animal rights. We also tend to become as blindly rigid as the jackal elders who dragged the woman before Jesus.

However, just as both young Daniel and Jesus were answers to an afflicted person's prayer, you can be one too. Let the words of this prayer be your intention on this Lenten Day:

> Make me, O God, an answer to another's prayer.
> Inspire me to act, being willing to turn on a dime,
>> to respond to someone in need,
>> so that, even unknowingly, I may become
>> an answer to the person's prayer to you.
> Keep me alert for all possible deeds of kindness.
> While hardly an angel,
>> by my Lenten alertness may I become
>> your angel of compassion and care.
> I rejoice in the great honor of that vocation
>> to be your response to another's cry for help.
> Grant me the grace to be an answer to a prayer.
> Amen.

Reflection

Examine your hands: Do you hold a stone that you would like to cast at someone or some group?

Whenever tempted to condemn another, consider performing this small ritual. First tightly clench your fist, as if around a stone.

Then release your clenched hand and symbolically drop the stone to the floor. Wipe your hands together as you pray, "Lord, have mercy on me a sinner."

O God, come to my assistance. O Lord, make haste to help me as I take up my Lenten allies, and my cross, to climb your holy mountain.

Fifth Tuesday in Lent

Moses makes a bronze serpent and raises it on a pole, and all who look upon the serpent are cured (see Nm. 21: 4-9).
Jesus tells the Pharisees that when the Son of Man is lifted up—like the serpent in the desert—all will realize his true origins and that God has not deserted him (see Jn. 8: 21-30).

If you find the act of inner cleansing to be unnecessary, reflect today on our Lenten mascot, the jackal dog. To the Egyptians, the jackal, in the form of the god Anubis, was sacred. Anubis was the guide dog who escorted the dead to the next world. The jackal-god was the patron of the mummification ritual and the priests who embalmed the dead. As the priests did their sacred work, they wore jackal-like miter hats.

Anubis was also the guard dog who sat at the gates of the next world. As the deceased approached, the jackal-god would sniff them thoroughly. If Anubis smelled evil, or blood, he would growl fiercely and block the entrance to paradise. Because of this test, when the Egyptians embalmed their dead, they placed sweet-smelling herbs inside the corpse.

The image of a divine jackal was not confined to the Egyptians. The name *Shiva*, the Hindu god of creation and destruction, means "jackal." The early gnostic Christians pictured Jesus wearing a jackal head. We can image a striking scene of Jesus as the Hound of Heaven, sniffing those who approach heaven's gates.

If we were sniffed today, would the Hound of Heaven growl at us? We might be tempted to answer, "No way! After these thirty-five days of Lenten penance, we're sweet-smelling! We've said our prayers, gone to church, performed pious works and kept the commandments. Why would the Hound of Heaven be snarling at us?" Yet are we sure there is no smell of evil, of blood, on us?

Alas, there is a smell of blood on our clothes. We might miss it, unless we examine our clothing closely, especially the labels. Smell your shirts or blouses as you read the euphemism on the label: "Tailored in Costa Rica" or "Sewn in Guatemala." In Guatemala alone there are over 600 garment factories which employ mostly women. These workers make one or two dollars a day sewing our clothing—if they're really fast, perhaps three dollars. In Guatemala, with its one hundred percent yearly inflation rate, it requires five to six dollars daily just to survive. The situation is compounded because garments entering our country from Central America require almost no import fees as long as the cloth to be sewn was sent there from the United States. Furthermore, in those South-of-the-Border Yankee sweatshops, physical and sexual abuse is common, but if you protest, you instantly lose your job.

Not only does our clothing smell of blood, so do our bananas! While bananas are Americans' favorite fruit, we don't grow them ourselves. In 1954, fifty-five percent of Guatemala was owned by the United Fruit Company of Boston—which also owned the railroads, the electric company and the telephone company. That was long ago—1954—and some things have changed. Yet a recent newspaper article reported a new contract that will solve one of our national problems. While receiving cheap clothing and bananas, according to that contract, we will ship to Guatemala twenty thousand tons of garbage daily. We've just found our new landfill!

Reflection

Look, today, upon the cross and the healing image of Christ that hangs on it. Ask to be forgiven for whatever share you might have in the oppression and exploitation of the third-world poor, who may feel that God has deserted them.

Caught in the web of international dependence for your clothing, food and gasoline, can you hide like an ostrich from your share in corporate sin? If you feel justified to condemn others of sin, considering yourself sinless, go to your closet and read the labels on your clothing.

Fifth Wednesday in Lent

Three holy men tell the king that even if God will not save them from the fiery furnace, they will not serve the king's god or worship his golden idol (see Dn. 3: 14-20, 91, 92. 95).

Jesus tells his followers that if they live by his teachings, they will truly be his disciples; knowing the truth, the truth will set them free (see Jn. 8: 31-42).

At midweek, we ponder the problem of how knowing the truth about our involvement in the exploitation of the world's poor can set us free. Lest the Hound of Heaven, Jesus as the Lenten Jackal, should sniff something unsavory about us, what can we do about the smell of blood—the sweaty smell of exploitation—on our clothing made by poor children and women? Knowledge of that reality can liberate us from the hypocritical belief that we are, as Jesus challenged the jackal-Pharisees, "without sin." The truth— all the implications about those shirts or blouses we wear—can free us if we can wear our third-world clothing like hair shirts.

Hair shirts were once the penance-garments of ascetics in the Middle Ages. They were a kind of "holy" underwear made from horses' hair, worn as a penance underneath one's usual clothing. One could be dressed in silk and velvet, and underneath be wearing a hair shirt. Wearing our clothes "tailored" in the third world as hair shirts can likewise make them into Lenten allies. We can let the labels scratch our necks and hearts as we put on those garments. A Lenten way to dress in them would be to put your hands upward through the sleeves as you pray that classic prayer: "O my God, I am heartily sorry for having offended you. And I detest all my sins because I dread the loss of heaven...." Put on your clothes with those hair-shirt labels in such a manner, and you will find it extremely difficult to hold a stone to throw at someone guilty of sin.

Find encouragement in the Gospel's good news about the woman caught in the sin of adultery: Jesus did *not* condemn her for her adultery! While that refusal must be a puzzling stumbling block to rigid, sin-obsessed Christians, it's good news to most of us. Jesus does not condemn us for our sins and failures; he only asks that we do not sin in the future.

There is no easy solution available for us. We live in such an interconnected world, where food, clothing and a wide range of our materials and products come from third-world countries. Awareness is a beginning, as is a willingness not to benefit from anything cheap if our gain means others' loss. Beware of all the shades of the sin of greed. Don't be a blind jackal, an "innocent" scavenger. Whenever we find a really good deal, what does that good deal usually tell us? Somebody's had a bad deal! A sign reading, **Close Out Sale! Everything 75% Off!** often says that somebody has lost a business! So don't walk in the store wearing a big smile and come home rejoicing. Come home mourning.

Like mountaineers, we are all roped together interdependently. The fate of our global expedition indeed depends on our ability to cooperate and care for one another. Always and everywhere, let us be careful not to practice profiting personally at someone else's expense.

Reflection

Instead of forgetting about your past mistakes and sins, let them become your itching hair-shirt reminders. Let your past sins remind you to never carry stones to throw at others.

Let your shopping, as a consumer in a global marketplace, awaken you to your share in oppressing the poor. There is a cost spiritually when others are impoverished so that you can live comfortably.

At each penance ritual you attend, remind yourself that you are indeed a sinner—even if you are only an abuser in the most general, global sense.

O God, come to my assistance. O Lord, make haste to help me, a sinner, as I take up my Lenten allies, and my cross, to climb your holy mountain.

Fifth Thursday in Lent

God tells Abram that he and all his descendants after him must keep God's covenant throughout the ages (see Gn. 17: 3-9).

Jesus solemnly assures the people that any who are true to his word shall never die (see Jn. 8: 51-59).

A common coat hanger is today's ally for us as Lenten mountain climbers in the ascent of the Mountain of God. Because we use hangers every day, we may be surprised that they could be a climber's ally. At the same time, it is because they are so common that they can serve as daily reminders on the rest of our Lenten ascent.

A hanger for a coat, shirt or blouse is useful because of its triangular shape. Likewise, every good spirituality is three-sided. Each of the sides represents one of the dimensions or beliefs of a sound spiritual lifestyle. One side of such a fruitful spirituality is morality, which involves the keeping of the commandments, loving one's neighbor and caring for the needy. The second side is our prayer-and-worship life—daily personal prayer and worship as well as communal and public expressions. The third side is an active awareness and involvement in the work of building justice and peace.

For centuries, Christian spirituality was only two-sided. Some spiritualities actually promoted complete noninvolvement in matters of social justice. Holiness was sought by retreating from the world so as to find God outside of the turmoils and conflicts of society. Those who still follow an otherworldly spirituality often strongly object to sermons on issues of justice and nonviolence. They believe firmly not only in the separation of church and state, but of religion and politics as well.

The ascent of these Lenten days is a mirror of our lives in the world. Part of the challenge of the new Lent is for us, as disciples of Christ, to make the cause of justice part of our daily lives. High atop this mountain we can hear the clear echo of God's words shouted by Isaiah as we departed from our base camp on Ash Wednesday. They speak about the only kind of penance that God desires: *releasing of those unjustly bound, setting free the oppressed, sharing your bread with the hungry, giving shelter to the homeless and clothing the naked* (see Is. 58: 5-7).

Therefore, together with our prayers and our efforts to be good people, we must also strive to ensure that people, not only in our country but anywhere in the world, have a right to decent wages, decent working conditions, food, housing and health care. Unless justice becomes an integral part of our lives, we will lack balance in our spirituality. Without the third side of the hanger of our holiness, we will lack what the Hound of Heaven is sniffing for: the odor of sanctity.

Reflection

Is your spirituality triangular? And if so, is it balanced? Does each side have equal or appropriate emphasis?

Guilt is a common response to an absence of prayer in your life or for some infraction of a moral law. Do you feel equally responsible for your failings to promote justice and equality for all?

Might it be spiritually useful to place another Lenten symbol in your prayer corner: a coat hanger?

Fifth Friday in Lent

Jeremiah tells us to sing to God with praise since God has rescued the poor from the hands of the wicked (see Jer. 20: 10-13).

When the crowds reached for stones with which to stone Jesus, he protested, asking them for which of his many good deeds they wanted to stone him (see Jn. 10: 31-42).

One week from today is Good Friday. This is a good day to ponder the cross of Christ with a parable:

A pious widow lived with her only son. She suffered from arthritis and also from the pain of a son who had lost his faith and was nonreligious. She prayed daily for his conversion as well as to be cured of her painful arthritis. For years she had longed to possess a relic of the True Cross, which she believed would cure her arthritis. The son ridiculed his mother's simple faith and pious devotion, which he saw as mere superstition.

On his way home one day, the son saw a large splinter in a fence post and brought it home. There he found an old gold pocket watch from which he removed the clock works. He laid the splinter on a piece of red velvet cloth, then placed it in the gold watchcase and closed its glass front. "Here, Mother, I just got this from Rome," he said. "It's a relic of the True Cross!" His mother was overcome with joy. She placed the relic in a place of honor in the living room, surrounded by countless candles.

Soon her living room became a neighborhood shrine where friends crowded to pray before the relic of the True Cross. The relic seemed to lessen the mother's arthritis. There were additional claims by friends of miracles and cures from various afflictions.

Months later at a local bar, the son told his friends what he had done, and they all laughed at the superstitious faith of such a silly religion. His friends convinced him to go home and tell his mother and her circle of pious friends the truth about the relic. The idea delighted him, but as he opened the door of the bar to leave, he found himself standing face to face with Jesus Christ! Jesus pointed a finger at him and said, "Stop! That splinter of wood you gave to your mother truly *is* part of my cross!"

The True Cross of Christ is the one on which today and daily his crucifixion continues. While that is true, so are today's words of Jeremiah. The prophet speaks of hope for the poor women sewing shirts and blouses in central America—that God will rescue them from the power of the wicked who exploit them. Sooner or later they will be rescued, as will all who suffer oppression—sooner, if we let our hands become God's hands.

Reflection

Look at your hands. Do you see them as extensions of God's hands? God needs your hands if those in need today are to be rescued.

Consider reaching out with your hands for your checkbook to send a donation to some worthy cause. Consider extending your hands to feed the poor as you serve at a soup kitchen. Creatively consider other ways today for how your common-looking hands can become the hands of God.

Take a few moments now to think about how you might be a part of the ongoing crucifixion and redemption of Christ.

O God, come to my assistance. O Lord, make haste to help me as I take up my Lenten allies, and my cross, to climb your holy mountain.

Fifth Saturday in Lent

The prophet Ezekiel gives us God's promise to cleanse the people and make them holy (see Ez. 37: 21-28).

After Jesus raises Lazarus from the tomb, the Pharisees and chief priests call a meeting of the Sanhedrin to decide on a strategy regarding Jesus. The high priest Caiaphas says that it is better to have one man die for the people than to have the whole nation destroyed by the Romans (see Jn. 11: 45-57).

This Mount of Olives, only two Roman miles from Jerusalem, is a critical location for the events of the coming week. In the village of Bethany on the east slope of the Mount of Olives, Jesus raised his friend Lazarus from the dead. The raising of Lazarus from the tomb is an overture to the great event of one week from now: God calling forth Jesus from his tomb after three days.

Today's Gospel presents a well-crafted, intricate scenario. For the religious authorities, the act of restoring Lazarus to life was the last straw. For giving life, Jesus now would lose his. Obviously, the loss of life usually means death, and so the climber's challenge of this Lenten Saturday is: Are we willing to die, even a little, that others may live?

Such sacrifice is cleansing. Recall what Jesus said about the woman who washed his feet with her tears and anointed them with precious perfume: that *much has been forgiven because she has loved much* (see Lk. 7: 47). Loving is the ultimate cleansing of sin. Love is the ultimate sacrifice, especially a love that refuses to count the cost of its gift.

The view from the Mount of Olives is of Jerusalem, particularly Mount Zion and Mount Moriah with its grand temple. Beyond the walls of the holy city rises the dark, ugly specter of Mount Calvary. Hidden from our sight by clouds is Mount Easter. The rising of Lazarus is for Jesus and for each of us a promise of what is hidden from view. Tomorrow, from this mount blanketed with olive trees the triumphant palm parade will descend into the Holy City. Tomorrow, we shall begin our final ascent as we enter into the days of Holy Week. Having come so far over these many days of Lent, it would be a shame now to waste the power of Holy Week.

We climbers need to be watchful on this slope, for we are traveling over a *scree*, a shifting slope made up of loose rock fragments and boulders. Be careful, for we can easily slip and fall back into the old Lent. Memories of old Lent and its sometimes morose and overly dramatic style of Holy Week can cause us to react like Sitting Bull's horse! When he toured with Buffalo Bill's Wild West Show, Chief Sitting Bull used a trick horse, which was given to him as a keepsake when he left the show. On the morning of December 18, 1890, the horse was tied outside Sitting Bull's cabin on the reservation when police arrived to take the chief into custody. The army had ordered his arrest as a precaution due to the revival of Native American fervor caused by the Ghost Dance.

In the confusion during his arrest—some historians say, intentionally—shots were fired and Sitting Bull was killed. His horse heard the shots and reacted as though they were the cue for his act. The horse began to do his tricks, sitting down and raising one hoof in the air. Astonished, everyone in the tribe thought that the spirit of Sitting Bull had entered his horse.

Conditioned by former years of Holy Weeks, we can react like Sitting Bull's horse. If we respond habitually to old cues of mournful music, readings of Christ's Passion and stark images of the cross, we can enter not into Holy Week but into a "Let's Pretend Week." We can piously pretend we are walking with Jesus in the palm procession and ascending the Mount of Skulls with him— and in the process missing the purpose of this holiest of weeks.

Reflection

Reject the temptation to jump from Sunday to Sunday, from the joy and victory of Palm Sunday to the victory and joy of Easter Sunday. Holy Week can indeed be holy for you if you spend it as a retreat week. Be zealous in applying a contemporary and personal application to each of the sacred memory events of Holy Week.

Plan ahead around your daily work and household activities so as to have free time for personal prayer, Scriptural and spiritual reading and reflection. Allot time as well to participate in communal parish liturgies during these coming holy days. Do whatever is necessary to ensure that next week can be prayerful. Let your climber's blue ribbon protect you from the temptation of being too busy to keep holy this week called Holy Week.

Tomorrow, we will arrive at camp three to pause and prepare for the final, most difficult ascent. As at camp two, this will be a place of decision about whether to continue climbing or to stop and descend. Today, pray for the grace to choose to be as completely involved as possible during these final, critical seven days. If you do so, you will know the victorious joy of having reached the summit of Mount Easter.

Palm Sunday
The Mount of Olives

The Suffering Servant says that he has set his face firm as flint. Since God is his help, he shall not be put to shame (see Is. 50: 4-7).

St. Paul tells us that our attitude should be like Christ's, who humbled himself as a slave and obediently accepted death, even death on a cross (see Phil. 2: 6-11).

Jesus begins his ascent to Jerusalem on an ass as the entire crowd of disciples shouts, "Blessed be he who comes as king" (see Lk. 19: 28-40).

After forty days of our ascent, the vision before us is a *massif,* a mountain with several well-defined peaks—the Mount of Olives on which we stand, and before us Mounts Zion, Moriah, Sauvage, Calvary and the highest peak, Mount Easter. The wind that blows across this massif that forms the summit of the sacred sierra carries the question, "Did Jesus know where he was going as he rode his donkey up to Jerusalem?"

Shouting *hosannas,* the palm-waving crowds who thronged after Jesus must have said, "He's on the right road. Where else would the Messiah go except to the royal city of Jerusalem to be acclaimed by the people?" The disciples must have added, "Well, at last, he's headed in the right direction. No more ambivalence about whether he is or isn't the Messiah. See, he's proudly proclaiming it to everyone!" The enemies of Jesus surely must have been gleeful over the palm procession. No more would they have to devise traps to ensnare him. Here Jesus was publicly proclaiming to be the Messiah. They knew the direction he was heading: up a dead-end street to a head-on collision with the twin powers of the Temple and the Roman Empire.

A perpetual question of travelers and explorers is, "Are we headed in the right direction?" At one time that question was answered by observing the stars or by following well-known landmarks. Travelers easily became lost if they strayed far from familiar landmarks or traveled in foggy conditions. After his baptism, Jesus took a dangerous journey into the desert and a personal confrontation with evil. He then traveled from the desert back to his hometown of Nazareth, there to be confronted not only by those in high places, but even by his neighbors and his own family. Without consulting the stars or looking for landmarks, a unique compass told him he was headed in the right direction, even as he rode that donkey up into Jerusalem.

On this Palm Sunday, do *we* know where we're going? We can easily feel disoriented in this turbulent age when old familiar landmarks, institutions and traditions are crumbling as in an enormous earthquake. Gone as well are former guidance systems, as radical and rapid changes occur in the areas of business, education, politics and religion. While we can be tempted to feel lost, let us find hope and direction by using the same compass Jesus used.

Jesus knew where he was going: to the center of the world, which for Jews and early Christians was located at Jerusalem. In ancient flat-world maps, a line drawn from each of the four cardinal points of the world intersected at Jerusalem. The intersection of those four lines formed a cross over the Holy City. It remained as the geographic center of their maps until the time of Columbus.

That cross with equal arms, a Greek Cross, is the most catholic—universal—of all religious symbols. This form of the cross was considered sacred by the ancient Celts, Chinese, Assyrians, Aztecs, Hindus, Greeks, Native Americans, and most pre-Christian peoples. Interestingly, early Christians did not use the cross as their sacred sign; for them the fish, lamb and shepherd were the most common images. The cross was avoided, for it was seen as a repulsive instrument of Roman torture and death. When Christians did embrace it, they chose the shape of the Greek Cross of equal arms.

When the Latin Cross, formed by a long upright bar and a shorter horizontal pole near the top, was proposed as the official Christian symbol, it was strongly rejected. Many of the early Church Fathers and theologians were horrified: "We will not have that pagan phallic symbol, the scepter of Apollo, as a sign of our religion!" By the seventh century, however, the Latin Cross was generally accepted, and by the ninth century it was universally accepted as the sign of Christianity.

Today, after the palm parade, we rest at camp three as the spring wind carries echoes of those disciples' *hosannahs* and the sweet smell of victory. To inexperienced climbers the ascent from here to Jerusalem on Mount Moriah and Mount Zion appears easy. It is not. It will be the most arduous part of all.

Mountains and climbs in general are classified in a universal system according to degrees of difficulty and the amount of technical equipment or expertise required. Classes one and two are like hiking over rough, steep terrain. With class three begins the need for ropes and other *assists*. In the coming days we shall move through class three and beyond, into situations that can bring about what climbers call *typewriter legs*. We may panic and freeze, and, like the clicking keys of a typewriter, our knees may shake with fear in the face of those heights that are saturated with the stench of death.

At this camp, as at our last one, those who shudder at the thought of climbing higher and risking their lives are free to leave the expedition and go back down the mountain. Is that your choice? You might also prefer to skip from the Palm Sunday Procession to the Easter Parade. If you decide to press on to the last stages of this ascent, however, you will need a compass. In the coming days of Holy Week we shall closely consider the unique compass that Jesus used—the one that we too should use.

Reflection

The cross, symbolizing Jesus' death and resurrection, is a

common sight. Latin crosses in gold or silver are worn around our necks. Crosses are placed in our homes and found on top of our church buildings. As the shadow of the cross falls across the days of this week, ask yourself what the cross means to you.

Today, the cross is a sign of the victory of Christ, a sign of his power. Yet the original implication of the cross, a symbol of defeat and death, can be of great value in these final days of the ascent. The cross as a sign of failure can remind you that God seems to prefer failure to success as the mysterious divine way of salvation.

The cross of shame and defeat is an anti-American sign since we greatly value winning over defeat, accomplishment over letting go. Yet consider tracing the sign of the cross over yourself in times of personal failure, defeat and disgrace as a reminder that God often prefers to use such times for your salvation. As you do, set your face as firm as flint, knowing that even in defeat and disgrace God is with you.

Monday of Holy Week

God's Servant is called by God for the victory of justice; God has grasped him by the hand (see Is. 42: 1-7).

Jesus tells Judas and the other disciples to leave Mary alone, saying that the precious perfume she poured on his feet was not wasted, that it was a preparation for his burial (see Jn. 12: 1-11).

"My burial"—Jesus' words to Judas, who objected to Mary's waste of money, indicate that he knew the direction in which he was heading: to the cross and his death. The cross was certainly his guidance system, one frequently consulted and referred to: "I must go up to the Holy City of Jerusalem; there I will be crucified and die!" To his disciples he said, "Take up your cross and follow me. Without the cross as your compass, you'll lose your way!" As a

100

pilgrim people—a name given to the church over thirty years ago by the Vatican Council—both the compass and the cross are fitting symbols of who we are.

A compass on a chain or cord could be worn around the neck in the same way as we wear a cross. It could remind us that while this is a turbulent age and we don't know where we're going, we're not lost! Along with the ropes and other special equipment we've begun to use since we arrived at camp three, today we are especially grateful for the compass. In these higher altitudes, sudden storms, clouds and dense fog can suddenly engulf us. Without a compass there's a real danger of losing our way, and even falling to our death.

The compass was a significant invention by the Chinese that radically changed all travel and exploration. Discovered between the eleventh and the thirteenth centuries, the Chinese called the compass, "the mysterious needle." By placing a magnetized needle in a bit of cork and floating it in a bowl of water, they discovered that the needle would always spin to the north! Lacking knowledge of the earth's polar regions and its magnetism, they did not understand how the magical needle worked, only that it did. Therefore, using the mysterious guiding needle required faith when travel was far from familiar landmarks or in dense fog. The use of the compass of Christ also requires faith, since the compass of Christ is the cross.

A classic compass is a "floating" Greek cross with one arm that points to the north. As a spiritual pilgrim, your cross is such a compass.

Reflection

Think of times when you've felt lost in the storms of life; then hold up the cross to them as your compass. See if that exercise sheds any new light on how you've gotten where you are and on your overall direction in life. Whatever the suffering you must face, see it as a sign that, as Isaiah said, God has taken you by the hand and is leading you to victory.

Whenever you are faced with a cross that points you down the road of shame, defeat and suffering, have faith in that direction.

As with the primitive compass or "mysterious needle," following your cross requires faith that the direction it points is God's way to salvation, to liberation and victory.

Check your cross-compass today. Do you feel you are headed in the right direction?

O God, come to my assistance. O Lord, make haste to help me as I take up my Lenten allies, and my cross, to climb your holy mountain.

Tuesday of Holy Week

Though the Suffering Servant fears that he has toiled in vain and used up all his strength, yet he still has faith that his reward is with God (see Is. 49: 1-6).

Jesus tells his disciples that one of them is about to betray him. Judas asks, "Is it I, Lord?" (see Jn. 13: 21-33, 36-38).

Judas refused to follow the compass of the cross, and so did the other eleven apostles—at first. That we are tempted not to follow the compass of our crosses is no reason to be ashamed. Pray for grace to follow the direction of the cross as we begin to scale the upper range of the sacred sierra, where angry storm clouds hide the summit.

Travelers and mountain climbers could easily walk around in circles without a compass. One of the main reasons we pilgrim people need a compass in our journey through life today is because there's so much fog. The fog has been created by the collision of two weather fronts. Thirty-some years ago, the warm winds of springtime reform swept over the church and the world, announcing radical change and renewal. Then about fifteen years ago, from another direction came the cold arctic winds of fundamentalism, orthodoxy and traditionalism. When those two fronts meet, one is invariably surrounded by fog. At high altitudes it's particularly dangerous, taking the form of *rime ice*, a freezing fog that settles on the rocks and makes footing treacherous.

Spiritual travelers in today's fog can suddenly come upon old forms of religious devotion and adoration, as well as old styles of religious dress. When these appear, it's natural to ask, "Didn't we leave that thirty years ago? Are we lost, walking in circles?" In today's rime-ice fog, a traveler might even come upon a reemergence of ugly anti-Semitism, with swastikas painted on synagogues. Puzzled, we ask, "What happening? That kind of hate was common fifty or more years ago! Why has it suddenly appeared again?"

Perhaps it's because we're feeling lost in the fog of conflicting religious positions and in the rapidly expanding possibilities of a changing world. We desperately reach out to reinvent old rituals and old structures which might affirm that there's solid ground in our lives. Travelers without a compass long for the foghorn of a strong authoritarian voice that says, "This is the way things shall be! This is what you are to believe! This is the way to go!"

Jesus had no strong authoritarian voice to guide him, only his cross-compass: "I shall go up to Jerusalem, where I will be tortured, suffer on the cross, die and rise again. Come, follow me." As disciples twenty centuries later, we are to follow in his footsteps— but there are no footprints on our road! To know the right direction, we must, like Jesus, follow the compass of our personal crosses.

Since there is variance between magnetic north pole and true north pole, compasses behave differently in different parts of the world and in different seasons. Because of this, periodic *variance correction* is required. Before leaving a recognizable point, a compass reading of magnetic north is checked against the present location's relation to true north on a map. Then a recalculation of the variance is taken according to the number of miles traveled since the last known landmark.

Distressing, even painful, is the awareness that there is no uniform compass direction in our personal crosses. A true direction in Rome or Paris may not be true in Tokyo. A spiritual *variance correction* is also needed. You can travel with confidence that your cross is an accurate compass if you check its direction in relationship to Christ's and adjust for the various cultural differences. The cross as a compass will point in different directions for different people—and different directions at various times and places in each individual's journey. Do not be fearful, however, for if you set your heart on the same goal as Jesus set his heart, you cannot lose the way.

Reflection

While some general rules can be given about morality and choices in life, can you learn to cultivate that infallible inner compass of a good and fully formed conscience?

The conscience-compass, magnetized by God's spirit, will lead you safely through the valley of death, the dark forest of fear and doubts, and the difficult desert of lonely decisions. With prayer, Scripture, reflection on tradition and good spiritual guidance, perfect your own inner compass of conscience. Then, regardless of what way it points, follow it with faith.

O God, come to my assistance. O Lord, make haste to help me as I take up my Lenten allies, and my cross, to climb your holy mountain.

Wednesday of Holy Week

The Suffering Servant says that he has not rebelled, has not turned back, for God is his help (see Is. 50: 4-9).

Jesus announces that a man who has shared his table is the one who will betray him (see Mt. 26: 14-25).

If the cross is our compass, then we know the way it points is always uphill and not down Easy Street. The cross always points through the thickets and thorns and up the hard road of sacrifice. This is the way that leads to loving-unto-death. Most people prefer to walk the way of loving only until it hurts. In life's painful situations the way of love is abandoned.

Penance is part of the life of a disciple, but good penance isn't wearing hair shirts or abstaining from food. The penance that bears real fruit is loving until it kills you. It's fitting that among ancient peoples, the cross was one of the great fertility signs. While the cross is an instrument of death, it is also a fertile sign pointing to the spring-like new life that flows from death.

When our compass-cross points to any one of the ten thousand small deaths that lie along the disciple's path, we must not reject it. Jesus experienced death in a friend's betrayal. Even Judas' kiss of death in the Garden of Olives was accepted by Jesus because he knew his compass pointed to Mount Calvary and the cross. While fearful, he didn't try to change its direction. Rather, with his faith anchored only in God, he let it lead him homeward.

Our cross-compass also points to an all-embracing new spirituality of the twenty-first century. Its open-ended arms reach out to both the East and the West, symbolizing the need for a fruitful blending of spiritual expressions. The cross's upward extension suggests a spirituality that points heavenward to the stars and beyond, to the furthest reaches of the cosmos. Its downward direction suggests a communion with all the earth and all creation.

As disciples, can we let our contemporary cross-compass lead us as Christ's led him? Is our faith strong enough to be able to let religious orders, ancient rituals and the traditions of our churches die as they go the way of Mount Calvary? Are we able to let all that we hold dear—our beliefs, our marriages, relationships and dreams—go the way of Calvary, with our faith anchored in the Pascal mystery of death and resurrection?

In these days of Holy Week, each time we look at a cross can we hear the voice of Jesus asking a question which echoes the title of the 1944 Academy Award-winning film: *Going My Way*?

Reflection

Every cross is a compass. Large or small, each calls you to follow Christ up the hard road of sacrifice. When your cross-compass points in that direction, do you follow it? When your cross points to a painful loving until it kills you, to a denial of self, do you follow it?

Consider purchasing a compass as a religious symbol. An inexpensive one can be bought in most drugstores or sporting goods shops. Place your compass on your desk or in your prayer corner, or carry it with you. Let it be a holy reminder that you are a pilgrim and explorer of the Divine Mystery who can frequently *feel* lost— but is really right on course.

O God, come to my assistance. O Lord, make haste to help me as I take up my Lenten allies, and my cross-compass, to climb your holy mountain.

Holy Thursday
Mount Sauvage

God's avenging angel is instructed to pass over the homes of those whose doorposts are marked with the blood of the lamb. Every home in Egypt is to be struck, but no destructive blow will come upon them. It is a day always to be remembered with a memorial feast (see Ex. 12: 1-8, 11-14).

Paul recounts Jesus' words of consecration: "This is my body, which is for you...This cup is the new covenant of my blood. Do this as a memorial feast of me." (see 1 Cor. 11: 23-26).

Jesus rises from the Last Supper table, ties a towel around himself and pours water into a bowl. Then he begins washing his disciples' feet, telling them that in his memory they must wash each other's feet (see Jn. 13: 1-15).

Without a doubt, today's ascent of the sacred sierra is on a class four route. From now on ropes and other *assists* are required because the path is nearing vertical. There will be many challenging areas and few shelves to rest on.

Towering above in the white light of the full moon of spring is Mount Sauvage. In the legends of the Middle Ages, on top of this mountain was the castle of the Holy Grail, making this the most legendary of all mountains. The Holy Grail was the cup used by Jesus at the Last Supper. Legend has it that Joseph of Arimathaea, standing at the foot of the cross, used it to catch the blood that flowed from Jesus' side as he died. Joseph is said to have taken the chalice to England where in time it disappeared.

Hundreds of years later, a nun in a convent—the sister of one of King Arthur's knights—had a vision of the chalice from the Last Supper. She told her brother of her vision and so began the quest for the Holy Grail, which was believed to have marvelous healing powers.

At the top of this mountain, however, we find no castle and no Holy Grail—only a plain upper room. While simple, the room is most significant since it was where Jesus chose to celebrate what would become the most important ritual of his community of disciples. For this meal of a new covenant he chose not a temple or a synagogue. This simple room lacks all the mysterious, awesome power of a cathedral and is devoid of the sacred aura of a church.

Being so plain and common, one would expect that the disciples' faith in what he said he was doing might be shaken. If the Memory Meal of Jesus, the Lord's Supper, were to be celebrated in the same kind of plain, familiar place, might not our faith also falter? Faith in supernatural happenings springs up easily when we are surrounded by religious images, statues, stained glass windows, gold vessels and the sense of awe surrounding sacred buildings. Whenever these are missing, the demon of doubt whispers in our ears, "Is what they *say* is happening really happening?"

Religious experiences are common in religious settings. Mystical experiences, on the other hand, come as unexpected visitations that usually occur in the most common of places and times. The French writer Charles Peguy said, "Everything begins in mysticism and ends in politics." When we look at the simple beginnings of the Memorial Meal of Jesus, and the beginnings of the church, those words of Peguy ring true. While with time the memory of that meal may have ceased to be mystical, the cup of that meal, the Holy Grail, grew in its mystical aura. Yet it's possible that all these years another legend connected to the Last Supper has been overlooked: the quest for the Holy Bowl used by Jesus to wash his disciples' feet.

In John's account of the Last Supper, that foot-washing bowl replaced the chalice as the sacred vessel! If that common bowl were found today, however, one wonders if it would be held with as much reverence as the mystical chalice used by Jesus. Yet, the bowl does have holy origins. For example, the Greek word for a sacred bowl is the same as the word for the container of blood within a woman's womb. From the womb of the washing bowl, Jesus brought forth a new sacrament: it was the birth of ordination to servanthood.

The ascent of Holy Thursday requires the steep climb beyond prestige to the humble ministry of servanthood as the arch-priesthood of Jesus' new covenant. It calls us to make the transcendental twist of rising not to power but ascending to the role of a humble servant. Only courageous climbers would consider undertaking such a difficult ascent. Hand over hand we climb the rope that leads up the sheer face of this mountain shrine of the Holy Grail and the Holy Basin.

Arriving at the top of a ledge, before us is an even greater leap of faith. We must cross a deep and narrow gorge, the *crevasse* of the consequences of the consecration of the Last Supper! Jesus consecrated the commonplace into the divine at that meal. The bread and wine of the meal, the drinking cup, washing bowl and even the room were made sacred—consecrated by the power of his love. No ordinary love, his was a loving unto death. To embrace the broad personal and mystical implications of the power of love to transform all creation is indeed a leap of faith.

In ages past, spirituality implied conducting one's life in a sacred manner. Living in a sacred manner means looking upon the ordinary with a mystical eyesight. When seen differently, the common things are soon handled in a different way—with reverence. During its first three hundred years, the church had no sacred buildings; it's members gathered for the Memory Meal in the plain rooms of their homes. Surely those rooms and homes were viewed differently as a result of the sacred meals celebrated in them. The table and vessels used to hold the body and blood of Christ surely must have been viewed in a sacred way—no longer treated casually. What if the intention of Jesus' commandment to repeat the memory of his sacred meal was not just to change bread and wine but the entire world?

Continuing to keep that memory is like throwing a pebble into the pond of the world to create an ever-widening circle of consequences that flows outward to the edges of the universe. If the sacred consequences and healing influence of the Eucharist seem to have been restricted, is it because we have restricted "Do this in memory of me" to the inside of church buildings? The grace and power of that Memory Meal indeed makes holy the church buildings where it is celebrated. However, was it Jesus' intention that churches or the *world* be consecrated?

In his book *Forgotten Among the Lilies*, the Canadian Oblate Ronald Rollheiser said this about the Liturgy of the Holy Eucharist: "The truly important consecration that takes place is the consecration of the people that are there." This belief was expressed long ago by St. Augustine. When he distributed Holy Communion, he would often say, "Receive what you are." Similarly, after his reception of Holy Communion, a friend of mine sits in his pew quietly repeating to himself as the rest of the communicants pass by: "The body of Christ...the body of Christ...the body of Christ...."

On this Holy Thursday, just like the first disciples, we struggle with the powerful implications of keeping the memory. There's a point in our reflection when we must grapple with the question: Do we wish to be consecrated into the body of Christ?

That question is never asked of the bread used for the Mass or Lord's Supper: "Would you like to be consecrated?" Imagine if the bread responded, "No. No, thank you. You see, I'm just ordinary daily bread, I'm only good for sandwiches! Besides, I wouldn't want to become the body of Christ—it might hurt!" At each Liturgy of the Holy Eucharist, each of us is personally asked, "Do you wish to be consecrated?" Unlike the blessed bread, we can refuse, saying, "No! I want to go to Communion, not *become* Communion!"

Reflection

Let this Holy Thursday feast of the Holy Basin of Humble Service grant you new eyesight. Look with reverence on your pots and pans, your brooms and brushes—all the vessels with which you perform the holy sacrament of service.

Can you see your humble daily service to family, friends and the world as another form of Holy Communion with Christ? Does your daily service to others, performed with great love, hold the same healing powers as the Holy Grail?

Today, or any time you attend the Lord's Supper, the holy Memory Meal, are you as willing to become as unreservedly consecrated as the bread and wine?

Good Friday
Mount Calvary

Isaiah tells us how it is our infirmities that God's Servant bears and our sufferings that he carries. Because he embraces his affliction, the Servant of God shall see the light of the fullness of days (see Is. 52: 13-53, 12).

Jesus carries his cross by himself, being led away to Golgotha, the place of the Skull. There they crucify him along with two others, one on each side (see Jn. 18: 1-19, 42).

Scaling to the height of this last Lenten Friday, we've gone beyond the class four routes. At such high altitudes, climbers frequently experience *mountain sickness,* an affliction brought on by oxygen deprivation, which causes headaches, nausea, disorientation, general weakness and even death. The first disciples, who accompanied Jesus on his ascent of this mountain, dropped out because of their mountain sickness, their weakness brought on by a fear of death.

Only the stouthearted dare to scale this class five Mount of Skulls and Bones. We have reached the summit of Mount Calvary as the sun hangs on the edge of the western horizon, only to find the crucifixion site now abandoned. Tomorrow is the great Sabbath of the Passover, and all have left for home. The Roman soldiers have departed, and gone as well are the bodies of the three crucified here. This mountain of death is deserted except for three ugly crosses.

As the setting sun, like a black hole, seems to soak up the

fading light of this day, the cross in the center looms high before us. On this forty-fifth day of our ascent, as we confront the mystery of the cross, let us reflect on the story of a Russian janitor. David Chakhvashvili disappeared in 1974 after being arrested by the Soviet police for impersonating a science professor. For years the unschooled but clever janitor had supplemented his small income by lecturing at a university on subjects like the atom, modern medicine and the technological revolution. He was good at what he did—but he was a fake.

Jesus challenges his disciples not to be fakes. We are called to an authentic discipleship by embracing the heart of the messianic way: suffering and the cross. Remember that forty-five days ago on Ash Wednesday, the instructions given us for ascending the Mountain of God were, "Unless you take up your cross and follow me, it is impossible to be my disciple."

When Jesus asked the apostles who the people thought he was, Peter affirmed boldly that he was the Messiah—God's chosen one. Yet when Jesus spoke of his death on the cross, Peter rejected the image of a suffering, cross-carrying, defeated and finally dead Messiah. As if waving an anti-demonic blue ribbon before Peter, Jesus reprimanded him with strong words: "Get away from me, you Satan!" Jesus dismissed Peter's image of him as the panacea for Israel's political problems. While a savior, he would not be some divine *Tylenol*, an instant cure-all for the headaches of slavery, exploitation, greed, war, poverty and oppression. Jesus refused to be seen as the kind of anointed one who would single-handedly heal the sufferings, burdens and pains of humanity and bring peace and harmony to the earth! If that is the image we hold of Christ as our savior, then we'd better look again. Christ rejects any notion of himself that excludes each of us carrying our crosses so as to share in his redemptive work.

England of the seventeenth century spawned some oddly creative religious writing. Consider, for example, this title: *Eggs of Charity, Layed by the Chickens of the Covenant and Boiled with the Water of the Divine: Take Ye and Eat.* Another book from that period was named *High-Heeled Shoes for Dwarfs in Holiness*. How accurately that seventeenth century author

113

described us twentieth century disciples! We're so often dwarfs in holiness, not for failing to pray enough but because we fail to carry our crosses. The favorite game of spiritual dwarfs in high heels is playing *Cross*, a game of pretend.

Pretending was a favorite game of Queen Marie Antoinette. She built ten thatched peasant cottages about a mile from her opulent palace at Versailles with its hall of mirrors and 1,400 splashing fountains. The queen installed some peasant families to live in them, and then she and her ladies-in-waiting would go there to play at being peasants. The queen would wear homespun garments, milk cows, churn her own butter and tend sheep. All this was so refreshing after the rigors of court life. Likewise, at the beginning of the twentieth century, the American millionaires, the Vanderbilts and Morgans, played at being hoboes. These very wealthy people would stage "poverty socials" in their grand marble mansions in Newport. Guests would arrive dressed in rags, eating scraps of food with their fingers from wooden plates and drinking beer from rusty tin cans.

Today, on Good Friday, we all can play *Cross*! As spiritual dwarfs, we can spend the day in mournful fasting and sorrow, but like Queen Marie Antoinette's playing, it's only for a day. Standing atop Mount Calvary in front of the empty cross of Jesus, ask yourself if you wish to play *Cross* or to embrace the cross? A cross can be embraced, and it can also be forced upon us against our will. However, before consciously choosing to embrace the cross, it's a good idea to review the various crosses found in the Cross Index, of which the following are only a sampling:

The Goat Cross: Some painful experience has been inflicted upon you by others as if you were a scapegoat forced to bear the scars of other's sinful actions. Those who carry a Goat Cross, in turn, usually blame their pain on their parents, teachers, their culture or the church. The Goat Cross is not T-shaped but V-shaped—standing for "victim." If this cross is carried, it is frequently carried into a courtroom along with a lawsuit.

The Crybaby's Cross: "Have pity on me, make exceptions for me and give me special treatment, for I am a disabled disciple. See the heavy cross I'm forced to carry in life!"

The Cranky Cross: Those who carry crosses are often cross. Because of their cross of sickness, overwork or family problems, they are crabby, irritable and short-tempered. Those who carry a cranky cross are crosses to others.

The Cross of Our Humanity: Be prepared to bear on your shoulders the cross of our human nature. Humans can be generous and also stingy, eager to serve and also self-serving, kind and also mean. Such is the imperfect nature of the human condition, and it's often hard to bear!

The Cross of History: We all carry the cross of a human history, which includes slavery, discrimination, violence, war, inequality between men and women and the greedy exploitation of the weak. As disciples of Christ, we must always be zealous for reform as we patiently carry the cross of the slow—the very slow—evolution of humanity.

The Criss-Crossed Cross: This cross includes the crosses of others. It is heavy with the sins and mistakes of your family, neighborhood and nation. This is a difficult cross to embrace since it is a sharing in corporate guilt and sin. It's hard enough to embrace our own sins, but to carry the sins of all with whom we are associated, including church, culture, and homeland is truly to walk in Jesus' path.

The Coppola Cross: In Rome in 1975, a young man named Roberto Coppola was arrested for impersonating a priest. For over two years he had performed numerous weddings, heard countless confessions and celebrated several hundred masses! Coppola told the arresting police, "What a shame to be arrested. I enjoyed being a priest. I so liked it!" The Coppola Cross is a way chosen by some who reject the Cross Road of Suffering. Similar to Marie Antoinette's and the Vanderbilts' games, it takes the shortcut of pretending. If Coppola so enjoyed acting like a priest, why didn't he embrace the eight years of hard study and all the daily burdens of being a real priest?

A form of the Coppola Cross of Pretending is frequently chosen by those seeking liberation from drug and alcohol abuse, marital problems or being overweight. Instead of the painful cross of embracing one's real suffering and thus changing one's lifestyle, an easier solution is sought: Can't you give me a pill, some instant cure-all for my problem? Instead of the Cross road of a painful but authentic resolution to problems, we like to seek shortcuts. We also like to look for a cross that's equipped with a parachute—so we can escape when the pain makes it too difficult to carry.

The messianic promise of a new era of justice and peace for all—especially for the poor and oppressed—will not come true simply because the historical Jesus carried his cross. You and I—all disciples—need to join him as co-redeemers, to embrace and carry our crosses, to deny our very selves as we surrender to God's will. The answer to the sins and evils of this world lies not in some instant cure-all, whether we hold up Jesus, the Bible or the church. The only cure is in the powerful medicine of the cross.

At the heart of the Good Friday liturgy is the ageless ritual of the Adoration of the Cross, in which we come forward to kiss the cross. Today, embrace your personal cross with great affection and love. When you do so, you can release from it the power to cross-fertilize and cross-pollinate humanity. Great is the power in each of our crosses to create a new breed of humans—not fakes, but true sons and daughters of God.

Reflection

If today, at this high altitude, your cross frightens you, take heart that Peter and the other disciples fled from Mount Calvary and Jesus' cross. Only later did they embrace their crosses. Pray for the grace to understand and embrace fully your cross on this Good Friday—and on every day that you are called to do so.

Can you accept your cross, realizing that God is a wise tailor, who has fashioned a unique and beautiful cross to fit you perfectly?

Can you also accept your cross as one of the essential elements in the divine formula for the healing medicine of the world?

Holy Saturday
Mount Pisgah

Hanging halfway up the face of the sheer cliff that leads from Mount Calvary to Mount Easter, we pause to survey the surrounding peaks below. Clinging for life to our ropes, we view the vast range of mountains before us as we prepare to continue our climb toward the summit. Today is tomb day, and as we look out over the mountain walls, we hear the echoing voice of the great Native American Chief Geronimo, who wanted to be buried on a mountain like this one. In his 1877 letter to President *Grant* he wrote of Arizona: "It is my land, my home...I want to spend my last days there and be buried among those mountains."

Below and to our left, rising up out of the clouds, is Mount Pisgah. Moses climbed that mountain with a heavy but grateful heart. In that sad mountain experience, God told Moses to go to the top of Mount Pisgah and look westward, northward, southward and eastward, to behold the Promised Land. Moses, however, would never cross the Jordan River and into the Promise (see Dt. 3: 27).

How bittersweet that Moses, who carried the heavy burden of the escape from Egypt and the forty years of the desert of Sinai, was not to enter Canaan, the land of milk and honey. It would be Joshua, his protégé, who would lead the people of God to inherit that promise. Moses, after viewing the Promised Land, fell dead on Mount Pisgah—perhaps more correctly, on Mount Nebo, which lies east of the River Jordan. Pisgah is used because in Hebrew it refers to the uppermost ridge of a mountain. On this Holy Saturday, by hard labor and difficult climbing, we have reached the uppermost ridge, the Pisgah of the sacred sierra of the Mountain of God.

Pisgah has come to mean any detached high point where one can view—briefly—the future but never enter into it. For us who carry the vision of Christ, it is Mount Pisgah and not Mount Easter that is our immediate destination! Like Moses, the great mountain climber of Sinai, we shall labor for a new era but will not likely see it accomplished in our lifetimes!

Rev. Martin Luther King has articulately spoken of Mount Pisgah: "I've been to the mountaintop, and I've seen the Promised Land. I may not get there with you!" It's a heroic symbol of those willing to give their lives for a dream, a promised tomorrow that they themselves will never enjoy. On Good Friday, even such a Pisgah view was not possible for Jesus from his cross, for it would have robbed Mount Calvary of its heart-crushing agony and deadly defeat that is essential to our redemption.

Now, however, on Holy Saturday, halfway between Mount Calvary and the summit of Mount Easter, hanging on for dear life to the ropes that connect us to one another, we view the path from Mount Pisgah. It's a perfect place to be on this tomb day of anticipation for the greatest of all feastdays, Easter. Yet Mount Pisgah is not shown on your map of the sacred sierra. That too seems fitting for this "empty" day of waiting—the only day of the church year on which the Eucharist is not celebrated—for even a glimpse of an unfulfilled dream does not often appear on the "maps" of heroines and heroes.

Blessed are those who have the conviction and courage to spend their lives laboring for any dream that they will never see realized in their lifetimes. Woe to those who give their lives to a work that can be accomplished within their lives, for they have sacrificed themselves for a little dream.

Reflection

Most of us seek instant rewards for our efforts at justice and peace. Do you feel a need to enjoy the harvest of your work before you die, if not right now? Do you have the courage to fast from gratification for your labors?

Can a Mount Pisgah vision be enough for you to give your life for a great dream? Can you, like Jesus, do without having a Mount Pisgah and have only a Mount Calvary—and still spend your life doing good? With or without a vision of the dream fulfilled, can you trust that your simple disciple's life is essential for the fulfillment of God's promised age of justice and peace?

Easter Sunday
Mount Easter

After the great flood, God promises to be with Noah's family and with all peoples and creatures of the earth—and seals the covenant with a rainbow (see Gn. 7: 1-13).

St. Paul advises that having been raised up in the company of Christ, we should now set our hearts on what pertains to the higher realms (see Col. 3: 1-4).

John's Gospel describes how before dawn, early in the morning of the first day of the week, while it was still very dark, Mary Magdalene came to the tomb of Jesus and found it empty (see Jn. 20: 1-9).

This morning in the predawn darkness we begin our final ascent. We cling tightly to the belay ropes that link us together—and to the knotted rope that has been set in *anchor mounts* driven into the face of the cliff. This climbing rope has been fastened on rings, or *carabiners*, by Christ who has climbed this way ahead of us. For the moment, all that we can see by the light of our helmet lamps is the rope directly in front of our eyes. In the dark we are aware that we have another companion: fear. Two thousand years of tradition assure us that victory awaits us at the summit, but that assurance is only possessed in faith.

For the past forty-six days your blue ribbon has been a symbol of protection from evil, and particularly the evil one. Fears are potent evil forces in our lives; they are the primary cause of the erosion of our faith. Two thousand years ago on the first Sunday after the full moon of spring, fears abounded. In the predawn darkness in the upper room, fear tied the little band of Jesus' male disciples in a knot. Fear had padlocked their hearts as well as the door to that room.

Fear gripped the hearts of not only the disciples, but also of Jesus' enemies, the Scribes and Pharisees. They feared that his followers would try to steal away the dead body of Jesus, and so they had guards placed at his tomb. The women disciples were fearful upon seeing the angels. They must have been fearful even before they left home, for graveyards were considered dangerous places because of the wandering spirits of the dead. Then the risen Christ appeared to the women, saying, "Do not be afraid."

Alpenglow, a mountaineering name for the rosy glow just before sunrise, begins to illuminate the slopes of this mountain. A radiance also rims the eastern horizon as we climb upward. If you look out, you can see far off in the distance, rising out of the clouds, Mount Ararat. It's the peak where Noah's ark finally came to rest after forty days of sailing in the great flood. This morning a faint rainbow rests above the peak of Mount Ararat, calling to mind God's solemn rainbow-sealed oath made with Noah and his descendants.

God's primal rainbow covenant with Noah is fulfilled in the resurrection of Christ. Just as God promised to be with all peoples, Easter is a feast not only for Christians but for all people; it embraces Jews, Hindus, Buddhists, Muslims and native peoples. It is a gift promised to the church of the covenant of Noah, which includes all the human family and all creation. Until the full light of dawn, all creation groans—even this mountain we are climbing—to share in the glorious resurrection of Christ.

While the summit remains hidden by clouds, from below rise the sounds of Easter sunrise, the peals of jubilant bells and alleluia-filled music. Do not let these sounds of victory tempt you to forget that fear is still with each of us on this final day of our ascent. In Matthew's account of the Resurrection, the women left the tomb, half fearful and half overcome with joy. Perhaps half-and-half is the proper Easter equation: half joy and half fear.

To take the edge off our fear, we are roped together as we

make the final ascent. We're steadily pulling ourselves up by the climbing rope that hangs down out of the fog and clouds around the summit. Paradoxically, this safety rope is interspersed with the large knots of our fears and anxieties beyond which we must pass. These knots have such names as cancer, AIDS, divorce and the loss of one's job or home.

Among the largest of the knots that confront us is the fear that we will lose our grip or that the belay rope connecting us will snap and we will fall to our death. The poet Milton spoke of that fear as a falling into "the dark womb of uncreated night." It's the fear of annihilation by death. Along our rope is also a large knot named *No Meaning*, an existential anxiety-knot that life's journey from cradle-to-grave lacks any ultimate significance.

As we climb higher on this rope—and as we grow older—we begin to encounter the knotted fears of having to live alone, being forgotten in old age, losing control, losing our driver's license—and so our independence—and ending our lives in a nursing home. John MacMurray writes that a cheap, second-class religion offers the pious message: "Fear not. If you love God and trust in God, none of those things you fear will happen to you." A good religion on the other hand says: "Fear not! All of those things you dread may very well happen to you! However, they're nothing of which you need to be afraid! With God's grace you will overcome each of them."

Looking up, we see that the clouds have parted from the summit, and a brilliant rising sun reveals a figure standing at the top of the summit: the risen Christ. "Do not be afraid," comes the voice of the Risen One. "Move over and beyond each knotted fear and keep climbing. Fear not, for perfect love, God's love for you and your love for God and one another, as perfect as you can make it, will banish fear." That message from the victor high atop Mount Easter's peak gives both hope and confidence to continue on this resurrection morning.

It is spoken by one who knows, since during his life Jesus knew every fear you've had or will have, being like us in all things but sin. In the garden of Gethsemani, Jesus was so fearful of his approaching passion that he sweat blood as he prepared to fall into "the dark womb of uncreated night." Take heart that he did not allow those knots of fear to prevent him from embracing his cross and his death. Jesus required his disciples to live lives of faith, and he himself placed a moment-by-moment faith in a God who does not break promises or covenants.

Easter is the feast of Baptism, the initiation into the mysteries of Christ's death and resurrection. Long before Christ, early peoples had special initiation rites into the mysteries of death and life, returning to and coming forth from the womb again. A Celtic pre-Christian ritual involved giving one end of a white cord or rope to those being initiated. The initiates were then lowered beneath the earth's surface into labyrinth caves which were called "purgatories." As they were left in the dark caves, they were told, "Follow the cord, and you will find your way out of this dark underground."

The cord they followed was a symbolic umbilical cord, a reminder of the cord that connected us to our mothers in the womb. The climbing rope we have been using in our ascent is also an umbilical cord that connects us to God. It connects us to our divine womb and parent from whom we have come and to whom we are returning. While there are knots in our sacred umbilical cord, they should not stop us, even if at times they seem too large to overcome and move beyond.

If today some large tangled knot blocks your ascent, don't give up. Don't attempt to untie it. Some of life's knotted fears can't be untied—being tied tightly inside our unconscious, we can't easily unknot them. Find courage in your faith, and pass over each knot in turn as you continue your ascent. Follow the rope-cord as you repeat with confidence the words of the master, "Do not be afraid. Remember, I am with you always."

At last, after forty-six days of climbing, we have reached the summit of Mount Easter. The vision of the Victor Christ in all his glory has disappeared, but in faith we know that he lives! The grandeur of the rising sun and the resurrection of Christ makes this Sunday the greatest of all feastdays and the overture to our personal resurrection from the dead.

On Ash Wednesday, as a member of this expedition, you

received a blue ribbon. Today is *the* day of the *cordon bleu*, the award acknowledging deeds of great heroism. Today you can wear the blue ribbon, the grand prize, with pride. You can pin it to your Easter bonnet or your suitcoat lapel since you have the distinguished honor of heroically making the ascent of the Mountain of God. Congratulations! Look upon your *cordon bleu* as your ribbon of honor as you stand on the height of Mount Easter in the fresh fertile wind of this first Sunday in spring.

The Conclusion
The Easter Road

Before you are the fifty days of Eastertide's celebration of the death, resurrection and ascension of Christ. Before you also is another route down from this mountain of victory.

Unlike ordinary mountain-climbing expeditions, we have not come here to plant our flag and then return! Recall the story about the Barrier Mountains of Australia that you read on the First Friday in Lent. The purpose of our Lenten expedition has not been to embrace our penances simply for forty days. Remember, while having reached the summit of Mount Easter, the path that leads back is not the way by which we came!

The Eastertide road leads another way into the brilliant light of a new day, down the opposite side into a new land. That road leads not to a new geographic place but rather to a new way of living. Not just the newly baptized but everyone who has made this difficult journey should now live in the new way of Christ. Your climbing allies, your disciplines and prayer life, were not temporary penances for past sins but useful tools of personal reformation. Having employed them for forty-six days, incorporate into your life the ones you have found of assistance.

Again, congratulations on your efforts in climbing and companionship during this great adventure. This expedition has been a training exercise for mountain-climbing disciples. Know that ahead of you in life are more and taller mountains, but also know that you've established a solid climbing pattern on this expedition. Make use of the knowledge learned in this Lenten ascent as you daily make your way ever upward to God.

As we each, by different pathways, prepare to depart, we wish one another, "Happy Easter and happy Easter living."

The Author

is a Catholic priest of the Archdiocese of Kansas City in Kansas. He was ordained in 1958 after eight years of education by the Benedictine monks of Conception Abbey, Conception, Missouri. He served as a parish priest for thirteen years and since 1972 has been the director of the Archdiocesan Contemplative House of Prayer.

Father Hays' writings include numerous books on contemporary spirituality and prayer, as well as parable stories. A pilgrimage to India and the Far East in 1971 has graced his writing with an inclusive religious spirit that also reflects the theological position of the Second Vatican Council.

The author has illustrated all his books but shuns the title of artist. Because of his love of art as well as his lack of any formal art education, he prefers to refer to himself as an amateur.

Author's Belay
Acknowledgment

For myself, being an author is akin to climbing mountains—in that it's not done alone. As a member of a team, a climber needs a belay, a rope, which secures him or her to companion climbers.

The writing of this book has been the work of a team of companions, each of whom in a special way has been a belay. They are more than friends—as members of the community to which I belong, they are truly companions.

First, I acknowledge **Thomas Turkle**, my publisher, who led the ascent by his strong encouragement, and his challenge to take on this task. I appreciate all his unseen efforts in the production and publication of this book. Closest to me on the belay-rope was **Thomas Skorupa**, my editor, who frequently shouted words of encouragement or warning. My next belay-ally was **Madelaine Fahrenwald**, who served as the team's technical editor since among her many gifts and talents is mountaineering.

Next along the lifeline of the ascent team were **Immanuel Eimer** and **Johnny Johnston III**, who along with Madelaine served as proofreading editors. They were belays to ensure that this book didn't slip into any one of numerous crevasses of incorrect English.

Along with these invaluable climbing companions was the support team of the other members of the Shantivanam Community to which I belong. The entire journey of the book, from the base camp to the summit, was made possible by their encouragement and logistical support. To each and all of them, I am indebted for their invaluable assistance.